The Harmonious Unity

The Harmonious Unity

Liu Zhi's Sino-Islamic Interpretation of the Five-Fold Path

by
Liu Zhi

Foreword by Wang Genming

Introduction and Translation
by Naoki Yamamoto

FONS VITAE

Published in 2026 by
Fons Vitae
49 Mockingbird Valley Drive
Louisville, KY 40207
http://www.fonsvitae.com

Library of Congress Control Number: 2026932039

ISBN 979-889640-0141

This book was typeset by Neville Blakemore, Jr.

Printed in the United States of America

Contents

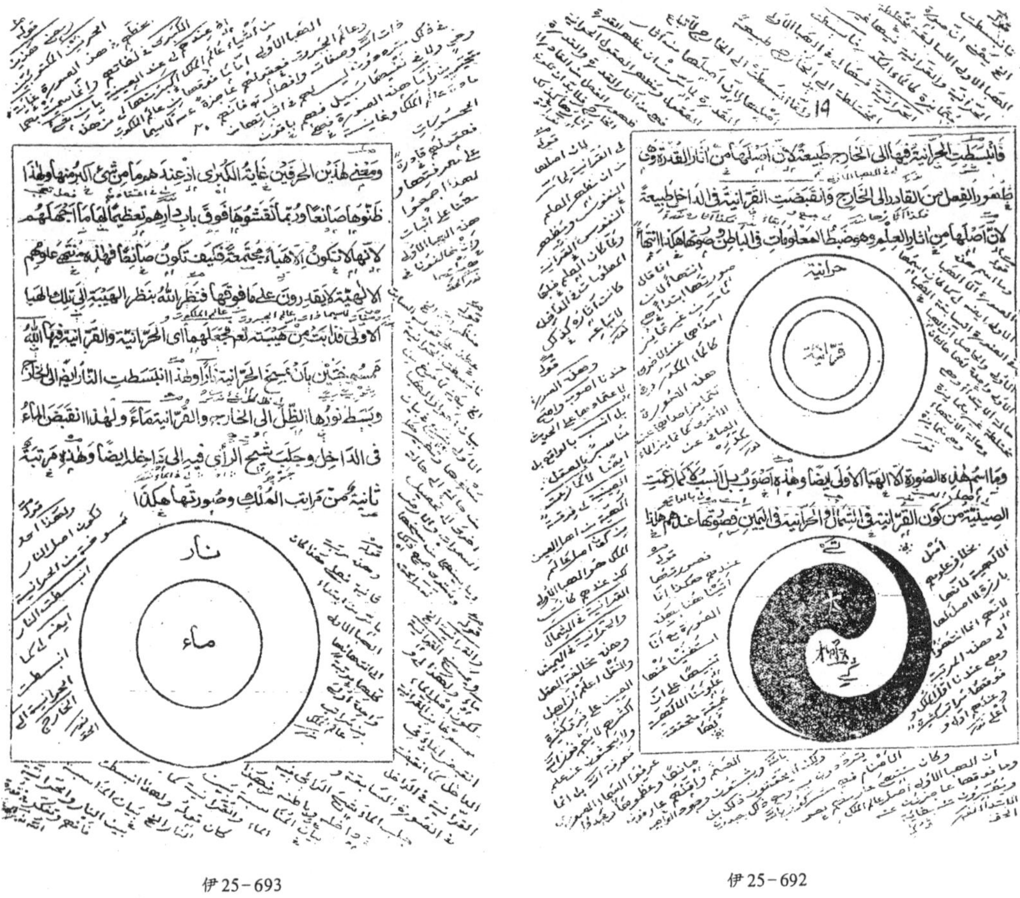

The Yin–Yang Diagram from the Arabic translation of Liu Zhi's *Tianfang Xingli*, together with its commentary, *Sharḥ al-Laṭā'if* by Ma Lian-yuan.

Foreword

I. The Author of *The Exposition of the Five Pillars of Islam* and Its Presence in Chinese Classic Literature

Liu Zhi's *The Exposition of the Five Pillars of Islam* ([五功释义]), first published over three centuries ago, remains one of the most influential Chinese-language Islamic works among the Hui Muslim community in China. Numerous editions have been produced over the years. More than four decades ago, I personally encountered a handwritten manuscript copy in a rural mosque, and during my childhood, I read and memorized parts of the text. Over twenty years ago, I began collecting various editions and eventually published a collated and annotated version (see *Annotated Teachings on the Nature and Principle of the Heaven* [天方性理校注], pp. 378–397, Religious Culture Press 宗教文化出版社, October 2020).

Below is a record of the editions of Exposition of the Five Pillars ([五功释义]) known to me, along with related biographical notes on the author.

An entry found on page 1788 of *Cihai* ([辞海], Compact Edition 缩印本, 1989), published by the Shanghai Lexicographical Publishing House (上海辞书出版社) in January 1990, reads as follows:

> Liu Zhi (ca. 1660–1730), an Islamic scholar of the early Qing period. Style name: Jielian (字介廉); in his later years, self-designated as Yizhai (一斋). A native of Shangyuan, Jiangsu (江苏上元, present-day Nanjing 南京), and a member of the Hui ethnic group. He first studied the Confucian classics, historical texts, as well as Buddhist and Daoist scriptures. Later, he delved deeply into Arabic and Persian, focusing on Islamic theology. His numerous writings and translations include such widely transmitted works as *Tianfang Xingli* ([天方性理], *Nature and Principle of the Heaven*), *Tianfang Dianli* ([天方典礼], *Rituals of the Heaven*), *Tianfang Zhisheng Shilu* ([天方至圣实录], *Authentic Record of the Most Noble Sage of the Heaven*), and *Exposition of the Five Pillars* ([五功释义]).

This entry marked Liu Zhi's and his *Exposition of the Five Pillars*'s ([五功释义]) formal entry into the field of Chinese academic scholarship. Later, *The Great Cihai: Volume on Religion* ([大辞海·宗教卷], December 2015, Shanghai Lexicographical Publishing House 上海辞书出版社) included even more detailed entries related to Liu Zhi and his works: "Liu Zhi" ([刘智], p. 600), "Tianfang Dianli" ([天方典礼], p. 668), "Tianfang Xingli" ([天方性理], p. 670), and "Tianfang Zhisheng Shilu" ([天方至圣实录], p. 671).

Between 1992 and 2000, several important Chinese reference works included detailed entries on Liu Zhi (刘智) and his translated or authored texts.

The Encyclopedic Dictionary of the Chinese Hui Muslims ([中国回族大词典], Jiangsu Ancient Books Publishing House 江苏古籍出版社, December 1992 edition) contains entries such as:

- "Liu Zhi" ([刘智], p. 941)
- "The Tomb Inscription of Mr. Liu Jielian" ([刘介廉先生墓碑], pp. 665–666)
- *Tianfang Xingli* ([天方性理], p. 895, *Nature and Principle of the Heaven*)
- *Tianfang Dianli* ([天方典礼], *Rituals of the Heaven*), *Tianfang Sanzi Jing* ([天方三字经], *Three-Character Classic of the Heaven*), *Wugeng Yue* ([五更月], *The Five Phases of the Moon*) and *Zhenjing Zhaowei* ([真境昭微], *Subtle Illuminations of the True Realm*) p. 896.
- *Tianfang Zhisheng Shilu* ([天方至圣实录], p. 904, *Authentic Record of the Most Noble Sage of the Heaven*)

The Comprehensive Dictionary of the Chinese Hui Muslims ([中国回族大辞典], Shanghai Lexicographical Publishing House 上海辞书出版社, January 1993 edition) includes:

- "Liu Zhi" ([刘智], p. 436)
- "The Tomb Inscription of Mr. Liu Jielian" ([刘介廉先生墓碑], p. 456)
- *Tianfang Dianli* ([天方典礼]) and *Tianfang Xingli* ([天方性理], p. 221)
- *Tianfang Zhisheng Lu* ([天方至圣录]) and *Tianfang Sanzi Jing* ([天方三字经], p. 223)
- *Tianfang Zimu Jieyi* ([天方字母解义], p. 224, *Explanation of the Letters of the Heaven*)

- *Exposition of the Five Pillars* ([五功释义], p. 235)
- *Wugeng Yuege* ([五更月歌], p. 236, *Song of the Five Phases of the Moon*)
- *Zhenjing Zhaowei* ([真境昭微], p. 816)

The Concise Dictionary of Islam ([伊斯兰教简明辞典], Jiangsu Ancient Books Publishing House 江苏古籍出版社, June 1993 edition) includes entries for:

- "Liu Zhi" ([刘智], p. 169)
- *Tianfang Dianli* ([天方典礼], p. 282)
- *Tianfang Xingli* ([天方性理])
- *Tianfang Zhisheng Shilu* ([天方至圣实录], p. 283)

The Annotated Bibliography of Chinese Islamic Texts and Translations ([中国伊斯兰文献著译提要], Ningxia People's Publishing House 宁夏人民出版社, June 1993 edition) contains extensive entries on:

- "Liu Zhi" ([刘智], pp. 605–606)
- *Tianfang Dianli* ([天方典礼], pp. 143–144)
- *Tianfang Xingli* ([天方性理], pp. 73–74)
- *Tianfang Zhisheng Shilu* ([天方至圣实录], pp. 39–41)
- *Zhenjing Zhaowei* ([真境昭微], pp. 83–86)
- *Exposition of the Five Pillars* ([五功释义], pp. 141–143)
- *Tianfang Zimu Jieyi* ([天方字母解义], pp. 293–294)
- *Wugeng Yue* ([五更月], pp. 339–343)
- *Annotated Explanation of the Three-Character Classic of the Heaven* ([天方三字经注解], pp. 342–344)

The Encyclopedia of Chinese Islam ([中国伊斯兰百科全书], Sichuan Lexicographical Publishing House 四川辞书出版社, March 1994 edition) includes entries for:

- "Liu Zhi" ([刘智]) and "Liu Zhi's Tomb" ([刘智墓], pp. 318–319)
- *Tianfang Dianli* ([天方典礼], p. 555, *Rituals of the Heaven*)
- *Tianfang Xingli* ([天方性理]), *Tianfang Zhisheng Shilu* ([天方至圣实录]), and *Tianfang Zimu Jieyi* ([天方字母解义], p. 556, *Explanation of the Letters of the Heaven*)
- *Wugeng Yue* ([五更月], p. 592, *The Five Phase of the Moon*)
- *Exposition of the Five Pillars* ([五功释义], p. 593)

The *Dictionary of Islam* ([伊斯兰教辞典], Shanghai Lexicographical

Publishing House 上海辞书出版社, October 1997 edition) features entries such as:

- "Liu Zhi" ([刘智], p. 483)
- *Tianfang Xingli* ([天方性理], p. 126)
- *Tianfang Dianli* ([天方典礼]) and *Tianfang Zhisheng Shilu* ([天方至圣实录], p. 127)
- *Exposition of the Five Pillars* ([五功释义]), *Wugeng Yue* ([五更月]), and *Tianfang Zimu Jieyi* ([天方字母解义], p. 128)
- *Tianfang Sanzi Jing* ([天方三字经], p. 129, *Three-Character Classic of the Heaven*)

The Comprehensive Dictionary of Religion ([宗教大辞典], Shanghai Lexicographical Publishing House 上海辞书出版社, August 1998 edition) contains entries for:

- "Liu Zhi" ([刘智], p. 469)
- *Tianfang Dianli* ([天方典礼]), *Tianfang Xingli* ([天方性理]), and *Tianfang Zhisheng Shilu* ([天方至圣实录], p. 802)
- *Exposition of the Five Pillars* ([五功释义]) and *Wugeng Yue* ([五更月], p. 869)

Among the aforementioned reference works, the *Encyclopedia of Chinese Islam* ([中国伊斯兰百科全书]) offers a relatively thorough and detailed exposition of Liu Zhi's life and scholarly contributions. Meanwhile, *The Annotated Bibliography of Chinese Islamic Texts and Translations* ([中国伊斯兰文献著译提要]) provides a more comprehensive and systematic explanation of his translated and authored works.

II. SUMMARY OF *THE EXPOSITION OF THE FIVE PILLARS OF ISLAM*

Exposition of the Five Pillars, in a single volume, is a foundational Hui Islamic text on religious rituals and institutional prescriptions. It is also referred to as *The Book of Rituals: Exposition of the Five Pillars* ([礼书五功释义]) or *Yizhai's Exposition of the Five Pillars* ([一斋五功释义]). The work was authored by Liu Zhi (刘智), a renowned Hui Muslim scholar of the Qing dynasty, whose sobriquet was Yizhai (一斋).

In this text, Liu Zhi employs the principles and terminology of Confucian moral metaphysics (性理学, *xingli xue*) to interpret and argue for the significance of the Five Pillars of Islam (五功) and their proper observance. The writing is concise yet rich in meaning, methodical in structure, and expansive in scope. As such, it has long been regarded by Chinese Muslims as a fundamental textbook for learning and comprehending the divinely ordained duties of Islam. Consequently, the book has been printed in many editions and widely circulated across generations.

The original date of publication is unknown, though it is generally believed to have been printed during the Kangxi reign (1662–1722) of the Qing dynasty. In the opening chapter, the author plainly declares his purpose:

> The Five Pillars of the Sacred Teaching—Declaration, Prayer, Fasting, Almsgiving, and Pilgrimage—are prescribed to guide humanity in cultivating the Way and returning to its original root. The Declaration is to know one's return; Prayer is to tread the path of return; Fasting severs attachment to worldly things; Almsgiving eradicates selfishness; and Pilgrimage fulfills the divine command and returns to the Real. By observing these, the Way of Heaven is fulfilled in its entirety.

The full text comprises approximately 30,000 characters.

The book is divided into sixty three chapters, symbolically reflecting the number of years the Prophet Muhammad (穆罕默德) lived in this world. Each chapter is composed of a concise essay of several hundred characters, bearing an individual title. The chapters can be grouped into three major thematic sections.

The first section consists of the opening seven chapters, which outline the origin and significance of the Five Pillars. These are summarized as follows:

- Chapter 1: The Origin – Asserts that the observance of the Five Pillars constitutes the fulfillment of the Heavenly Way.
- Chapter 2: The Principle – Describes how human beings are stained by five forms of sensual desire: sound, color, scent, taste, and touch. The Five Pillars serve to counteract these attachments and resolve the resultant afflictions.
- Chapter 3: Love and Aversion – Argues that the Pillars cultivate in a person the ability to love what is good and abhor what is evil, thereby enabling the establishment of public virtue and the suppression of selfish desire.
- Chapter 4: The Outer Senses – Discusses the external sense

organs (the "five officials") and their moral capacities. The Five Pillars serve to restore virtues already lost and preserve those yet unspoiled.

- Chapter 5: The Inner Virtues – Identifies five internal virtues in the human being. The function of the Pillars is to purify selfish impulses, rectify vital energy (气), balance discernment between right and wrong, stabilize strategic thinking, and restrain emotional extremes of joy and sorrow, gain and loss.
- Chapter 6: The Virtues of Heart and Nature – Expounds the tripartite division of human qualities: in nature there are the five classical virtues – benevolence, righteousness, propriety, wisdom, and faith (仁, 义, 礼, 智, 信); in the emotions there are joy, anger, love, aversion, and desire (喜, 怒, 爱, 恶, 欲); in cognition there are memory, recollection, speech, calculation, and operation (忆, 记, 语, 筹, 运). To function rightly in the world, each set of five must be harmonized in moderation, and the Five Pillars serve precisely to correct imbalance and return each to its proper equilibrium.
- Chapter 7: The Balanced State and Distorted Change – Explains how humans are born with four innate dispositions and are composed of the Five Elements (metal, wood, water, fire, earth). Vital energy governs their harmony. When this energy becomes disordered, virtues are distorted into vices: brilliance becomes arrogance and lust; humility becomes flattery and wantonness; steadiness becomes obstinacy and sluggishness; honesty becomes dullness and ignorance; gentleness becomes indolence and apathy. The Five Pillars, then, are the means by which vital energy is cultivated, enabling the maintenance of a state of perfect equilibrium among the Five Dispositions.

From Chapter 8 to Chapter 32, the author devotes twenty-five chapters to a detailed exposition of the specific regulations pertaining to the Five Pillars. This section approaches each of the Five Pillars—Declaration of Faith (念), Prayer (礼), Fasting (斋), Almsgiving (课), and Pilgrimage (朝) – through five analytical dimensions: ritual form (仪), legal prescription (法), moral obligation (义), metaphysical principle (理), and proof of truth (证).

From Chapter 33 to Chapter 63, a total of thirty-one chapters, the author expands upon the meanings of the Five Pillars by exploring their religious, moral, and social significance from multiple dimensions. This final section of the book elaborates on the comprehensive, transformative implications of the Five Pillars in human life.

- Chapter 33: The Five Devotions – Explores how the Five Pillars restrain excessive attachment to worldly affairs, reminding believers of the origin and end of life, and curbing greed and indolence.
- Chapter 34: The Gatherings – Argues that communal prayer binds individuals together; the weekly congregational prayer is termed *gathering*, and the two annual festival prayers constitute *assembly*. Assembly governs gathering, gathering governs the community, the community governs the individual, the individual governs the self, the self governs one's nature, and nature governs the heart.
- Chapter 35: The Counsel of Worship – Explains that praying together yields seventy times the merit of solitary prayer; thus, collective worship is essential.
- Chapter 36: The Measure of Worship – Details the numeric structure of daily worship: 32 bows, 64 prostrations, 178 praises, 12 hand-raisings, 17 kneelings, 32 uprisings, 27 offerings, 11 right-and-left glances, 5 proclamations, and 5 benedictions—totaling 384 acts, corresponding to the numerological principles of cosmic creation and solar division.
- Chapter 37: The Symbols of Worship – States that the postures of prayer imitate the forms of Heaven, Earth, and all creatures.
- Chapter 38: The Origins of Worship – Asserts that the five daily prayers were instituted by Prophets, from Adam to Muhammad.
- Chapter 39: Sincerity of Heart – Emphasizes that the aim of performing the Five Pillars is *sincere intention* and *moral resolve*.
- Chapter 40: The Five Symbols – Declares that among the Five Pillars, the Declaration of Faith is primary, as all other pillars revolve around it.
- Chapter 41: The Gates of Virtue – Describes the Five Pillars as the gateway to virtue, the steps to ascend to Heaven, the

path to subtle truths, the essence of all beings, the vessel to cross the sea of life, and the foundation for cultivating self and nature.

- Chapter 42: Drought and Rain – Portrays the Five Pillars as rain in drought, a spring in thirst, a lamp in darkness, a cloud at noon, and a remedy in illness—granting peace amidst adversity.
- Chapter 43: The Five Blessings – Summarizes their effects: the Declaration reaches the divine, Prayer defeats Shayṭān, Fasting extinguishes desire, Almsgiving removes hardship, and Pilgrimage severs worldly attachments.
- Chapter 44: The Five Breaths – Explains the Five Pillars as a ceaselessly circulating cycle, without beginning or end.
- Chapter 45: The Transformations – Claims the Five Pillars participate in the creative processes of Heaven and Earth, in harmony with yin and yang.
- Chapter 46: Unceasing Practice – Cites the sage for whom the Five Pillars are seamlessly integrated: *engages in remembrance of the Divine without conscious effort, worships without bending the body or bowing the head, fasts without renouncing food or desire, gives alms without distributing wealth or grain, and performs pilgrimage without facing a specific direction.* This, however, does not mean abandoning the practice, but rather attaining its essence. Even saints of the highest inner realization continue to uphold the Five Pillars.
- Chapter 47: The Whole Body – Shows that the Five Pillars engage the entire human body: some are enacted in the heart, others in the limbs.
- Chapter 48: Belonging and Intent – Aligns the Five Pillars with bodily faculties and the Five Elements: Declaration to fire and the heart, Prayer to earth and the body, Fasting to wood and the will, Almsgiving to water and knowledge, Pilgrimage to metal and intention.
- Chapter 49: Forgetfulness and Aspiration – Echoes the theme of Chapter 46, discussing the purification of delusion.
- Chapter 50: Opening of the Senses – Argues that the Five Pillars awaken human perception, exemplified through the lives of Prophets.
- Chapter 51: The Effects of Devotion – States that, as the sages say: "Through the cultivation of the Pillars, Heaven and

Earth are drawn into harmony"; and as the Prophet says: "To reach the utmost is to reach the Divine."

- Chapter 52: The Three Ultimates – Describes the Five Pillars as encompassing Heaven, Earth, and Humanity—the three cosmic realms—and asserts they provide a single, unified path through them.
- Chapter 53: The Symbols of Law – Discusses humans as the meeting point of Heaven and Earth, the basis of yin and yang; the Five Pillars are thus most fully expressed in the human being.
- Chapter 54: Constant Virtue – Proposes that the Five Pillars perfect the virtues of life and destiny, unite Heaven and Man, and fulfill the constants of human conduct.
- Chapter 55: The Role and Power of the Five Pillars – Explores how the Pillars connect human affairs with divine workings, reveal hidden causes, penetrate the mysteries of nature, and clarify the meaning of life and death.
- Chapter 56: The Universal Principle – Describes the Pillars as encompassing Heaven and Earth, exceeding the ordinary and embracing the sacred, uniting men and women, embodying the cosmos, and reflecting all beings, even the divine.
- Chapter 57: The Sacred Law – States that the Pillars embody the legacies of past Prophets, serve as models for later ones, are commanded by the True Lord, conveyed by Prophets, and taught to humankind. Following them is to embody the divine and imitate the saints.
- Chapter 58: The Ladder of Law – Declares the Five Pillars to be the lawful path ascending toward Heaven, with layered stages that cannot be skipped or rushed.
- Chapter 59: Simplicity and Depth – States that the way of the Prophet is both simple and profound, immediate yet far-reaching; it is presented with clarity and taught with earnestness.
- Chapter 60: Position and Nurture – Proclaims that by fulfilling the Way of Heaven and completing human relations, one achieves spiritual maturity and full cultivation.
- Chapter 61: The Sacred and the Common – Asserts that saints become saints through the Five Pillars; the virtuous imitate them; the wise understand them; the ignorant neglect them—this is the dividing line.

- Chapter 62: Loyalty and Filial Piety – Argues that to serve one's parents without diligence in the Pillars is not true filial piety; to serve one's ruler without reverence in the Pillars is not true loyalty.
- Chapter 63: Tawhid – Concludes that the Five Pillars unify principle and refine human nature, improving the character of ordinary people.

Although the Five Pillars are the foundational rites of Muslim life, the author approaches them not merely as ritual obligations, but as a profound gateway into the doctrines and spiritual philosophy of Islam. Through multi-faceted analyses of their origin, function, requirements, and religious significance, Liu Zhi offers a deep and nuanced exposition of Islamic teachings.

Rather than adopting a general tone of advocacy, the author engages in layer upon layer of excavation and reflection—chewing over every concept, weighing every word, carefully examining each facet. Building upon the insights of earlier scholars, he distills his own understanding into each of the definitions and explanations, embedding his personal theological reflections throughout. The result is a text of exceptional conciseness and philosophical depth, where each line offers clarity at a glance and insight upon reflection.

Furthermore, the language of the text is rich in vocabulary and rhythmic in cadence, making it both intellectually engaging and aesthetically pleasing when recited. The overall structure is meticulously organized, and the prose exhibits a refined literary quality.

One especially striking feature appears in Chapter Seven: The Balanced State and Distorted Change, where Liu Zhi's dialectical mode of thought comes vividly to light. In this section, he analyzes how inherent human dispositions, when unbalanced, mutate into their opposite extremes, and how the Five Pillars serve to restore harmony. This expression of dialectical reasoning (辩证思想) reveals a remarkable depth of insight, marking the chapter as one of the most intellectually compelling in the work.

III. A Survey of Editions of *Exposition of the Five Pillars*

Since its initial publication, *Exposition of the Five Pillars* has appeared in several major printed editions, extending into the Republican period. These include the Guanzhong edition from the third year of the Jiaqing reign (1798, 嘉庆三年关中刻本), the Huanchuntang edition from the Daoguang era (道光年还淳堂刻本), the Gui family's Danyutang edition from the first year of the Xianfeng reign (1851, 咸丰元年桂氏丹腴堂刻本), the Fudetang edition from Xianfeng nine (1859, 咸丰九年福德堂刻本), and two editions from the Republican era: one by Guo Nanpu in the ninth year (1920, 九年郭南浦刻本), and one by Ma Fuxiang in the eleventh year (1922, 十一年马福祥刻本).

In *Tianfang Dianli* ([天方典礼]), volume five, in the first general entry, there is a note: "For details, see *Exposition of the Five Pillars*" (详见[五功义]), indicating that *Explanation* must have been completed no later than *Tianfang Dianli*. Yu Kai's *Preface to Liu Yizhai's Exposition of the Five Pillars* ([刘一斋先生五功释义序]) was written in the forty-ninth year of the Kangxi reign (1710), suggesting that the text may have already been completed and printed by that time. The original edition may have been the Zhongzhou Yazhengtang edition from the thirty-third year of the Qianlong reign (1768, 清乾隆三十三年中州雅正堂刻本), printed by Mai Changfa and Wang Yong'an. Other editions include the Jinling Qichengtang edition from the fortieth to forty-third years of Qianlong (1775–1778), printed in Nanjing by Yuan Guozuo; and the 1859 edition engraved by Ma Qingshan Renzhai of Hexi (河西马青山仁斋氏刻本).

The Toyo Bunko (Oriental Library) in Japan houses a Republican-era reprint from the Wanquan Book Company in Beijing (1920, 民国九年北京万全书局重排印本), which has not been seen in mainland China.

A lithographic edition is included in volume 15 of *The Great Encyclopedia of Islam* ([清真大典]第十五册), consisting of the lead-type edition printed by the Beiping Qingzhen Press (北平清真书报社铅印本, pp. 伊15–249 to 伊15–263). The text begins under the heading "The Book of Ritual: Exposition of the Five Pillars" ([礼书五功释义]). This edition is prefaced by two introductions: one by Li Tingxiang dated to the eighth year of the Republic (1919), and another by Ma Kuilin, who notes that the reprint was done by "Ma Fuxiang of Yunting, Longyou" ("陇右马福祥云亭氏重印"). It contains more than ten marginal notes, hereafter referred to as the "Ma Fuxiang Annotated Edition" (马福祥本注).

According to Ma Kuilin's reprint preface, dated the 19th day of the twelfth lunar month of 1919:

> When this book was first translated, it was not engraved at the time. In the Qianlong year of *wuxu* (1768), Mai Changfa and Wang Yong'an of Zhongzhou raised funds to create woodblocks, thus enabling publication. Unfortunately, the engraving was careless, resulting in many errors that confused readers and led some to disregard the book—an injustice to Liu Zhi's original intent. Later, Luo Danquan of Shangdang, passionate about religious education, oversaw a careful re-engraving. However, since the blocks were kept in Shangdang, those living far away found it difficult to obtain printed copies. Witnessing this, I spared no personal expense to print another thousand copies, so that those devoted to the Way could study it thoroughly.

The Zhongzhou edition from Qianlong *wuxu* (1768) is likely the original print. The Luo Danquan edition is not extant. The lead-type edition in question was printed in a run of 1,000 copies.

In 1948 (Republic 37), Daoist leader Min Zhi of Lintan published a stand-alone edition in Lanzhou, based on this lead-type edition, retaining only the main text and notes. In 1988, the West Hall of Lintan reprinted this stand-alone edition. It is finely produced with clear characters. By contrast, *The Great Encyclopedia of Islam* edition combined two pages into one for cost-saving, making the notes difficult to read.

The Complete Collection of Hui Classics ([回族典藏全书]) includes two versions:

> Version 1 is found in volume 25, pp. 319–386. It is labeled as a Qing woodblock edition (清木刻本) and includes references to "republication by Ma Qingshan Renzhai of Hexi" and the title "The Book of Ritual: Exposition of the Five Pillars" ("河西马青山仁斋氏重刊""礼书五功义"), suggesting it may be the 1859 Xianfeng edition.

> Version 2 is in volume 26, pp. 1–32, and is a lead-type edition bearing the phrase "Reprinted by Ma Fuxiang of Yunting, Longyou" ("陇右马福祥云亭氏重印"), likely corresponding to a 1926 reprint.

Selected and Continued Editions of Chinese Islamic Texts ([中国伊斯兰教典籍选续编]) volume 8, pp. 4479–4585, includes a composite lithographic edition titled *Commentary on the Nature and Principle,*

Exposition of the Five Pillars, and The Five Phase of the Moon ([性理注释 五功释义 五更月歌三种], 民国二十年五月铅印), which includes a preface by Ma Fuxiang and a postscript by Ma Shucheng. Additionally, there is a reprint by the Zhonghua Book Company in Shanghai (November 1931, 民国二十年十一月), also marked as "Reprinted by Ma Fuxiang of Yunting, Longyou".

A modern typeset edition appears in *The Collected Works of Hui Muslim Classics* ([中国回族典籍丛书], 文白对照, vol. 5, pp. 631–665), with a modern Chinese translation included on pages 665–707. Another version is included in *Annotated Teachings on the Nature and Principle of the Heaven* ([天方性理校注], Religious Culture Press 宗教文化出版社, November 2020, pp. 255–282).

A recent edition of *Exposition of the Five Pillars*, with annotations and translation by Liu Peilun (刘佩伦), was published during Ramadan 2024 by the Committee on Sinicized Qur'anic Exegesis of the Zhengzhou Islamic Association. It consists of the original text, notes, and modern Chinese translation, in total 126 pages.

IV. Conclusion

From the foregoing overview of its various editions and textual features, it is evident that *Exposition of the Five Pillars* is a work of clear and accessible content, with wide and enduring influence. There is no need for me to elaborate further or embellish its significance with excessive words.

Wang Genming (王根明)

Acknowledgment

I would like to thank Neng Dong, Mariam Tam, Heng Wang, Dr. Ibrar Bhatt and Dr. Wang Genming for their help with proofreading the translation.

While proofreading the translation, we referred to Mr. Ma's modern Chinese translation and commentary.

The translation is based on 劉智「五功釈義『回族典藏全書』第２６冊、pp. 4-35.

Naoki Yamamoto

Introduction: Liu Zhi's Way of Islam

His life

Liu Zhi, styled Jielian (介廉) and known by the sobriquet Yizhai (一斋), was born around 1670 C.E. into a family of Islamic scholars (Akhung) in Nanjing. His father, Liu Sanjie, was a preeminent scholar who played a central role in Nanjing's Muslim community. Such was his reputation that even Ma Zhu, another prominent figure in Chinese Islamic history, sought him out to review his writings. Liu Sanjie's erudition in Islamic studies was widely acknowledged and respected.

During his early years, Liu Zhi received his education in the madrasas of Nanjing, where he was also deeply influenced by his father's scholarly pursuits. At the age of fifteen, Liu resolved to dedicate himself fully to the path of learning. For the next eight years, he immersed himself in the study of Chinese classical traditions, followed by six years devoted to Islamic classics, three years to Buddhist texts, and a year to Daoist studies. He further read an impressive collection of 137 Western classical works, achieving a mastery that positioned him as a true inheritor of both Eastern and Western traditions.

However, Liu Zhi's voracious reading was not driven merely by the pursuit of knowledge for its own sake. Rather, it was aimed at delving into the profound depths of "Tianfang" (Islamic) learning. His ultimate goal was to elevate Islamic scholarship to the status of a "universal discipline," a treasure shared by all under heaven. Through this synthesis of diverse traditions, Liu Zhi became a scholar of unparalleled breadth and vision, seeking not only to enrich his own understanding but to establish a broader intellectual and spiritual foundation for Islamic thought within China.

After the death of his father, Liu Zhi's dedication to scholarship only deepened. He distanced himself from all human relationships, devoted nearly all his resources to his studies, and retreated to a humble hermitage in the mountains, where he immersed himself in intellectual pursuits. By the time he reached his mid-forties, twenty-eight years had passed since he first resolved to pursue a life of learning at the age of fifteen.

However, Liu came to realize that merely reading classical texts and indulging in solitary contemplation would not suffice to uncover the essence of Islamic scholarship as a "universal learning." Determined to expand his understanding, he left his hometown of Nanjing, carrying his provisions on his back, and wandered across the vast landscapes of China. According to Liu, he visited more than half of China's renowned cities, traveling through Shandong, Beijing, Hunan, Hubei, Shaanxi, Suzhou, Hangzhou, and beyond. During these journeys, he sought out Muslim scholars in each region, learning from them, identifying the shortcomings in his own writings, and refining his ideas through rigorous intellectual exchanges.

Upon returning to Nanjing, Liu Zhi eventually established a distinctive style of Islamic scholarship deeply rooted in the soil of Chinese intellectual traditions. He pursued what he called the "Three Axes of Knowledge," a study of the True Lord (Allah), the cosmos (macrocosm), and humanity (microcosm), emphasizing their interconnectedness.

Yet, despite his unparalleled vision and unique scholarship, Liu Zhi struggled to gain the recognition he deserved, not only within China's intellectual circles but even among his fellow Muslims. In the preface to his biography of the Prophet Muhammad, *The True Record of the Most Sage of Islam* (*Tianfang Zhisheng Shilu*), Liu Zhi confessed the profound loneliness that haunted him:

> "I have no companions in life, nor any colleagues in work. Even my family and close friends consider my lack of engagement in productive labor to be an ill omen."

> "I write my manuscripts myself, transcribe them myself, edit them myself, and refine them myself, yet I dare not affirm them myself."

> "I have searched every bookstore for books on Heaven, Earth, and Humanity, only to find words that are stale and devoid of substance."

> "I know no moment of peace. My brothers and relatives regard me as foolish and eccentric, avoiding me and distancing themselves from me. At one point, I had to move several times within a single year."

The renowned Hui Muslim writer Zhang Chengzhi reflects on Liu Zhi's isolation, suggesting that his solitude was emblematic not just of his personal struggles but of the broader plight of Islam—and religion in general—in China:

> "This [anguish of loneliness] might be recognized as the solitude of Islam in China, and indeed of religion itself in the Chinese context. Confronted with the harsh realities of life, the overwhelming power of the state, and the vast ocean of Chinese culture, any religion that seeks to remain faithful to its principles will find itself confined to loneliness, with its very survival at risk. In the blood-soaked history of Hui Muslims during the Qing Dynasty, Liu Jielian's writings become all the more astonishing with each reading." (Zhang Chengzhi, *China as Seen through Islam: Ethnicity, Religion, and the State, Chuko Shinso*, 1993, 58 p)

The classical Islamic works from China that we hold in our hands today are the fruits of relentless dedication, forged by Chinese Muslims who, undeterred by isolation, sought to reveal the truths of Islam as a "universal discipline." Their uncompromising spirit endures as a testament to their pursuit of the divine.

The "Dao" of the Five Pillars of Islam: Liu Zhi's Vernacular Articulation of Islamic Spirituality

> "The Five Pillars serve as the pathways of cultivation, guiding humanity toward harmony with Heaven (the divine truth). The first is the practice of Dhikr (Remembrance of the True Lord), the second is the act of Salah (Rendering reverence to the True Lord), the third is the discipline of Sawm (Fasting as an act of purification), the fourth is the virtue of Zakat (Charity through giving), and the fifth is the journey of Hajj (Pilgrimage to the sacred sanctuary). These Five Pillars are not merely commands of the True Lord but are practices exemplified by the Prophet as a model for all humankind, providing a clear and universal path to spiritual harmony." Liu Zhi, *Tianfang Dianli*

In the realm of Chinese Islamic thought, the use of East Asian vocabulary to articulate Islamic philosophy is not a mere instance of superficial cultural syncretism. Rather, it represents the outcome of profound philosophical and theological ingenuity. Chinese Muslim thinkers employed traditional East Asian concepts and linguistic frameworks not only to convey the fundamental doctrines of Islam but also to reinterpret these teachings within the intellectual paradigms of East Asia.

The notable characteristic of this synthesis is the redefinition of core East Asian philosophical concepts—such as li (理), qi (気), and xing (性)—within the framework of Islamic thought. For instance, li, a concept central to Confucian and Daoist traditions, is reconceptualized in Islamic terms as a manifestation of divine will and universal truth. It comes to signify the order and law that the Creator has embedded within all of creation. Similarly, qi, traditionally understood as the dynamic energy or life force animating the cosmos, is reimagined in Islamic terms as the sustaining principle through which God governs and maintains existence.

A second defining feature of this intellectual endeavor is the sophisticated deployment of East Asian vocabulary to elucidate the ethical and ritual practices that form the core of Islamic teachings. Foundational practices such as prayer, fasting, and almsgiving are reinterpreted through the frameworks of harmony between tian (天: Heaven), di (地: Earth), and ren (人: Humanity), as well as the cosmological principles of yin-yang and the five elements. For example, prayer is presented as an act of standing before Heaven, prostrating upon Earth, and embodying the cosmic balance of the universe. Through this redefinition, Islamic practices resonate deeply with East Asian perceptions of nature and humanity, rendering them more accessible and relatable to the cultural sensibilities of the Chinese audience.

Liu Zhi's Study of the Three Axes

Drawing upon the vernacular lexicon of East Asia, Liu Zhi sought to present the Islamic tradition as "the universal learning" accessible to both Muslims and non-Muslims within the Chinese intellectual and cultural milieu. To achieve this ambition, Liu Zhi redefined the Five Pillars of Islam as a profound wisdom that completes the harmony among the "Three Axes" of Heaven, Earth, and Humanity.

In Liu Zhi's philosophical framework, the "Three Axes"—Heaven, Earth, and Humanity—represent the three fundamental realms of existence: the cosmic, the natural, and the human. These realms are not viewed as separate or isolated but are deeply interconnected through the practical observances of the Five Pillars. Liu Zhi's vision weaves together these axes to form an integrated path for understanding human life and its ultimate purpose.

The harmony of Heaven and Earth is realized through the practice of the Five Pillars, which embody the universal principles of divine order and manifest them within the material world. These observances align the spiritual and physical realms, thereby fostering a balance that transcends the dichotomy of the temporal and the eternal.

Humanity is situated as the unifying axis that bridges Heaven and Earth. Through the Five Pillars, individuals cultivate themselves, drawing closer to the divine essence of Heaven while simultaneously contributing to the moral and social order of Earth. Humanity becomes the living testament of this unity, embodying divine will and earthly responsibility in harmonious concert.

When the balance of the Three Axes is achieved, the entirety of existence functions as a seamless cycle of interconnectedness. Heaven, Earth, and Humanity operate as one unified whole, enabling individuals to actively participate in the cosmic order. Such harmony, Liu Zhi asserts, is not merely an abstract ideal but a lived reality that can be realized through the disciplined application of the Five Pillars.

This study of the Three Axes in Liu Zhi's thought reveals a vision of humanity's place within the cosmos, wherein the divine, the natural, and the human converge. His work thus offers a profound synthesis of Islamic spirituality and East Asian intellectual traditions, portraying the Five Pillars as the means by which this tripartite unity is brought to fulfillment.

The Wisdom of Heaven

In Liu Zhi's philosophical framework, the "Wisdom of Heaven" refers to the exploration of the fundamental principles governing the cosmos and the universal laws that underpin them, with a focus on how these truths can be embodied in human life and action. This study is constructed around the principles of order, harmony, and creation symbolized by Heaven, encompassing a worldview that manifests as the will of God (Allah).

In the realm of Heaven's wisdom, the universe is understood not as a mere collection of material phenomena but as a domain imbued with the creative intent of God and the laws deriving from it. Heaven represents the embodiment of divine law, and its inherent order is reflected in the workings of nature and human existence. The interplay of yin and yang, the cyclical movement of the five elements, and the transitions of the four seasons are all seen as manifestations of divine will, underscoring the harmony and stability of the cosmos.

This "Heavenly Principle" (理) finds its tangible expression through the Five Pillars of Islam: Testimony of Faith (Shahada), Prayer (Salat), Fasting (Sawm), Almsgiving (Zakat), and Pilgrimage (Hajj). In remembrance, Heaven's tranquility and unshakable stability are embodied as the heart turns toward God, seeking connection with the cosmic center. Prayer symbolizes the harmony of Heaven and Earth, aligning human actions with divine order through the reverent use of the body. Fasting reflects Heaven's purity and detachment, guiding individuals to curb their desires and draw closer to divine intent.

Almsgiving mirrors Heaven's selfless virtue, embodying the act of bestowing blessings without expectation of return, and becomes a means through which divine principles are realized in human society. Pilgrimage, in turn, serves as a symbolic return to the cosmic origin, an act that reconnects humanity to the beginning and end of all creation, reaffirming its essential purpose.

Of particular importance in the study of Heaven's wisdom is the necessity for humans to not merely comprehend these laws but to embody them in their daily lives and actions. Liu Zhi asserts that by mastering the principles of Heaven, individuals can refine their inner virtues and foster greater harmony and order on Earth. This perspective illustrates that Heaven's principles are not confined to natural phenomena but are deeply intertwined with human spiritual development and societal stability.

Moreover, Heaven's wisdom underscores the idea that the universe is an integral part of divine creation, offering humanity the opportunity to rediscover its role within this sacred whole. While transcending human existence, Heaven serves as a reflective plane for divine order, realized through human deeds. Thus, the study of Heaven becomes a philosophical framework of immense scope, linking the will of God with human action and aspiring toward universal harmony on a cosmic scale.

The Wisdom of Earth

Liu Zhi's intellectual framework, the "Wisdom of Earth" constitutes a study of the material world and the foundation of human life, exploring how the cosmic order (as articulated in the Wisdom of Heaven) manifests within human society and the natural environment. Earth, as the realm of God's creation, serves as the domain where the principles of Heaven actively operate. For Liu Zhi, the Wisdom of Earth plays a bridging role, linking the universal laws of Heaven with the practical actions of humanity in a concrete and actionable manner.

Earth symbolizes both God's bounty and humanity's responsibility. It encompasses the mountains, rivers, land, flora, fauna, and human society itself, representing diverse expressions of the Earth's symbolic dimension. Each of these phenomena operates according to divine laws established by God, and humans are similarly expected to align their lives with this order. This adherence to cosmic and natural law forms the core of the Wisdom of Earth.

A central theme within the Wisdom of Earth is the harmonious relationship between humanity and nature. For instance, the Five Elements (Wood, Fire, Earth, Metal, Water) and the interplay of yin and yang are understood as principles that maintain balance on Earth. Liu Zhi emphasizes the importance of refraining from destructive desires and actions, advocating for respect toward the cycles and laws of nature as a foundational teaching of the Wisdom of Earth.

Furthermore, the Wisdom of Earth extends into the social realm. Ethics, institutions, and rituals within human society are closely connected to practical elements rooted in Earth's principles. The Five Pillars of Islam, for example, serve as essential tools for establishing social order. Prayer reinforces communal solidarity, Zakat alleviates poverty through the sharing of wealth, and fasting fosters self-restraint, promoting social harmony.

The Wisdom of Earth also seeks to actualize the principles of Heaven through everyday activities such as agriculture, commerce, and governance. Liu Zhi argues that through such practical endeavors, humans can lead lives aligned with divine will. In this sense, the Wisdom of Earth is not a purely theoretical pursuit but a pragmatic discipline that provides a clear pathway for humans to harmonize their actions with Heaven.

Another crucial aspect of the Wisdom of Earth is its emphasis on the Earth as a nurturing ground for human growth and fulfillment. Earth supports life, fosters growth, and simultaneously serves as a testing ground for cultivating human virtues. Liu Zhi posits that by living and engaging with nature and society in accordance with divine will, humans can spiritually mature and ultimately achieve true harmony with Heaven.

Ultimately, the Wisdom of Earth, grounded in the principles of Heaven, elucidates the material world and humanity's role within it. It acts as an intermediary domain, harmonizing practice and ideal, and seeks to fulfill divine will through earthly existence. This philosophy integrates the metaphysical and the practical, guiding individuals toward a life that mirrors the unity and order of the cosmos.

The Wisdom of Humanity

In Liu Zhi's "Wisdom of Humanity" centers on the essence, role, and moral development of human beings. It elucidates humanity's responsibility as the bridge connecting the universal laws of Heaven and the material foundations of Earth. This discipline seeks to explore how human beings, endowed with their innate nature (性) by Heaven, can fully realize their potential and align themselves with the cosmic order through the cultivation of the Way (道).

Connection with East Asian Concepts of Cultivation

Liu Zhi's conception of the "Wisdom of Humanity" aligns closely with the East Asian traditions of self-cultivation. In Confucianism, Daoism, and Buddhism, the ultimate goal of self-cultivation is to refine the self and achieve harmony with Heaven, the Dao, or Buddha-nature. Similarly, Liu Zhi emphasizes that human beings, through the practice of self-discipline, can live in accordance with the divine laws of Heaven. This intellectual synthesis represents a unique fusion of East Asian and Islamic thought.

The Essence and Role of Humanity

According to Liu Zhi, humanity is bestowed with an innate nature (性) by Heaven, one that is inherently pure and virtuous. However, living within the material world of Earth, humans are prone to desires and emotions that obscure their true nature. Consequently, self-cultivation is necessary to refine this nature and restore its original purity. Central to this process of refinement are the Five Pillars of Islam (五功), which serve as the foundational practices for human self-cultivation.

For example, dhikr, or remembrance of God, involves quieting the mind and focusing on the divine. This practice resonates with the Confucian concept of jing (敬, reverence) and the Buddhist notion of meditation (zenjo), as all emphasize inner stillness and attentiveness. Similarly, prayer integrates physical action with spiritual alignment, harmonizing the body and mind while expressing humanity's connection to Heaven. These practices represent disciplined paths through which humans can govern themselves and maintain inner balance.

The Importance of Practice in Self-Cultivation

As with East Asian traditions of self-cultivation, Liu Zhi's Wisdom of Humanity emphasizes the importance of practical engagement alongside theoretical understanding. The Five Pillars provide a concrete framework for integrating the principles of Heaven and Earth into human life, thus enabling individuals to fulfill their potential. Each of the pillars plays a distinct role in this process:

> Shahada: This practice directs the heart toward God and purifies thought, restoring inner purity. It parallels East Asian practices of introspection and self-reflection, which guide individuals back to their true essence.
>
> Prayer: Through physical gestures of reverence, prayer connects humans with Heaven, facilitating a state of alignment between body, mind, and the divine order.
>
> Fasting: Abstaining from physical desires helps to remove distractions and achieve spiritual purification, curbing impulses that disrupt harmony.
>
> Zakat: Acts of charity transcend material attachments and promote social harmony by fostering generosity and ethical engagement with others.
>
> Pilgrimage: The journey to sacred places symbolizes a spiritual return to the source, transcending the material self and achieving higher spiritual growth.

The Integration of Heaven, Earth, and Humanity

Liu Zhi extends his analysis of human self-cultivation to include those who internalize and embody these practices. He refers to such individuals as "Perfected Individual" (至人), those who continually practice the Five Pillars with sincerity and vigilance. These individuals integrate body, mind, and spirit, aligning their lives with the principles of Heaven and achieving harmony with the natural world and society.

Through the Wisdom of Humanity, Liu Zhi portrays human beings as unifying agents who connect the laws of Heaven and the material realities of Earth. By acting in accordance with divine will and practicing virtue in their worldly lives, humans can achieve both individual fulfillment and collective harmony.

Liu Zhi's Wisdom of Humanity presents a distinctive synthesis of East Asian traditions of self-cultivation and Islamic teachings. It emphasizes the refinement of human nature and the harmonization of Heaven and Earth, placing the Five Pillars at the heart of its practical framework. This discipline offers a holistic vision of spiritual growth and universal order, serving as a bridge between East Asian and Islamic thought and providing valuable insights for contemporary discussions on spirituality and ethics.

念

物　花

課　為

The Exposition of the Five Pillars of Islam

by
Liu Zhi

The Exposition of the Five Pillars of Islam

Introduction

In the beginning, there was the Supreme Ultimate. And from this, the two primal forces of Yin and Yang were born. When the two principles came into existence, the Four Symbols (the four stages) were established. With the establishment of the Four Symbols, the Five Elements then arose. These Five Elements generate one another and overcome one another in eternal harmony. Likewise, in the sacred laws of Islam, there are five essential duties: Shahada, Salat, Sawm, Zakat, and Hajj.

These Five Pillars mirror the order of the cosmos, for just as the Five Elements govern the workings of the world, so do these five duties govern and sustain the soul's journey.

These duties, like the Five Elements, are indispensable, and the principles of generation and overcoming are woven into their very essence. To generate means that from them the true nature of being is born, and to overcome means that by them the desires of the self, which arise later, are driven away. All depends upon the intention of the individual. If one's intention is grounded in truth, then by performing these five acts, that truth will naturally be revealed. But if one's intention is fixed upon mere form, then only the outward form will be seen.

As it is often said, the virtuous behold virtue, the wise behold wisdom; the deep-hearted perceive depth, and the shallow discern only shallowness.

Now, Master Liu Zhi has sought to investigate the meaning of the Five Duties one by one, delving deeply into their very source. Furthermore, he has extended these principles to encompass related matters, so that scholars of future generations, through diligent study and the unification of body and mind, might not only grasp what has already been spoken, but also, through analogy, understand what has yet to be said. Thus, the Five Duties are not merely confined to five acts alone.

The numbers of Heaven are five[1], and likewise, the numbers of Earth are five[2]. The five positions are in harmony with one another, each bound by its own connection. The total of fifty-five[3], the numbers of both Heaven and Earth, is derived entirely from the principle of the Five, upon which all is founded and proceeds.

Thus, by embodying these five acts, observing them with precision, and diligently carrying them out, one may ascend from the foundational learning to higher understanding, through the long-accumulated truths. By rigorously disciplining oneself, one will at last arrive at the realm of silence, where words are no longer needed. This is the very vision that Master Liu ardently hoped for in the world, and it is his wish that the people never forget his intent, but faithfully carry it forward.

In the 49th year of the reign of Emperor Kangxi, in the third month of the year Gengyin, this was written beneath the light of a lamp. Composed by the disciple of the faith, Yu Kai.

The Rites of the Pure Faith

Faith has long been divided, yet the truth of Islam runs deep. Heaven, Earth, and Man—the Three Powers—are governed by the workings of creation, and the Five Offices preside over all things. What does the Limitless (Wu Ji) truly encompass? There is a God, though He is beyond all definition. In stillness, seek the profound and mysterious truth, and with sincerity, follow the guidance of the Lord.

The Purpose of the Pure Faith

To remain unsullied and keep to purity is to safeguard the truth at its very source. With unwavering sincerity, one illuminates even the most subtle matters. In loyalty and filial piety, there is no other design, nor does one tire of advancing these principles time and again. Though there is nothing to gain, one holds it close to the heart, desiring only to share the rare and precious treasures of wisdom with others.

1. Numbers of Heaven refer to odd numbers, namely 1,3,5,7,9.
2. Numbers of Earth refer to even numbers, namely 2,4,6,8,10.
3. The sum of the numbers of Heaven (1+3+5+7+9) and the sum of the numbers of Earth (2+4+6+8+10) make 55.

Chapter 1: The Origin

When form and energy manifest, the Heavenly Way (the cosmic order) becomes veiled. As energy arises daily, the truth is obscured. What is clear becomes concealed, what is pure is mingled, and the paths of understanding are blocked. Mankind, unaware of the source of their divine mandate, knows not whence they came, nor how to return. Yet the Five Duties of Islam—the Pillars of Faith—offer a way: Shahada, Salat, Sawm, Zakat, and Hajj. These guide humanity in the way of cultivation, restoring them to their original purity.

Shahada is the knowledge of where one's devotion belongs. Salat is the practice of that devotion upon the path. Sawm severs the ties of worldly desire, and almsgiving teaches the soul to forget itself. Hajj is the fulfillment of the divine mandate and the return to truth. Through the mastery of these duties, the path of Islam is fulfilled, and the soul returns to its rightful place in the order of all things.

Chapter 2: The Principle

The Way of Heaven and the heart of man, though subtle, are intertwined. Allah, in His Wisdom, has granted a single principle to all things, yet the manner in which people receive it differs. Thus, there arises the distinction between the sage and the ordinary man. The Sage (the Prophet), through the Law, guides all creation, and the truth of the Way (Dao) is clear to him. But the ordinary man, seeking to grasp the Way through material things, finds that the truth is obscured.

For this reason, they cannot recover the truth and return to their original state of purity. Therefore, Allah has commanded the Five Pillars, revealing to humanity the path to cultivation. The Five Pillars open the barriers, clear the obstructions, show the way forward, and lead man back to his original state.

What are these Five Pillars? The heart and nature of man are bound together, much like a key and its lock. Man's ears, eyes, mouth, nose, and body are immersed in the five sensations of sound, color, scent, taste, and touch. From these arise the five desires of love and hatred. The spring of these desires becomes entangled with the key, tightly wound, and impossible to release. But if one uses the correct key, perfectly suited to the lock, the spring and key will be released naturally.

The human body is bound by the chains of these five sensations, and thus it is that the five laws (the Five Pillars) must be used to address them. In doing so, the bonds are gradually loosened, the heart is clarified, and one's true nature is revealed. In this way, the truth of the Law becomes clear. This is why the Five Pillars are of utmost importance in the cultivation of the Way.

Chapter 3: Love and Aversion

The ear is attuned to sound, the eye to color, the nose to scent, the mouth to taste, and the body to touch, each in its proper accord. Yet love inclines towards what is beautiful, and aversion recoils from what is foul—thus, in this regard, they are the same. But to be without love or aversion, without the perception of beauty or ugliness, and to follow purely the law of Heaven (the cosmic order)—this is the virtue of justice.

To accept only what one desires without discerning whether it is truly worthy of love, or to hate what one despises without examining the cause—this is a virtue tainted by selfishness. But to know the flaws within what one loves, and to recognize the beauty within what one despises—this is the virtue of clarity.

The governance of man by the Five Pillars—faith, prayer, fasting, almsgiving, and pilgrimage—is to conquer selfish desire, restore the virtue of clarity, and ultimately return to the state of perfect justice, where all is impartial and without bias.

Chapter 4: The Outer Senses

The five senses, each endowed with its own function, possess within them their own virtues. Yet man, as he is, fails to fully realize the goodness inherent in them. The mouth is endowed with the virtue of speech, the ear with the virtue of hearing, the eye with the virtue of sight, the nose with the virtue of smell, and the body with the virtues of grasping, moving, and resting. In these virtues, there is no inherent evil, but if they are used improperly, their virtues are lost.

The Five Pillars of Islam are ordained to restore the virtues that have been lost, and to preserve them from further loss, ensuring that the faculties of man remain in their rightful purpose and harmony.

Chapter 5: The Inner Virtues

Within man there are five inner virtues: nature, heart, wisdom, inclination, and subtlety. Nature is the essence of life, heart is the faculty of perceiving, and wisdom is the means by which one applies these. Inclination is the movement of the heart, and subtlety is the hidden state of the heart. That which is revealed when the heart begins to move is called "sign," and that which remains concealed is called "subtlety."

These five virtues are originally pure and perfect gifts bestowed by the Creator (Allah). Yet selfish desire clouds one's nature, disputes bewilder the heart, temperament obscures wisdom, schemes unsettle the stirrings of the heart, and joy, anger, gain, and loss disturb its hidden depths. Thus, what is inherently good flows toward what is not good.

The principle of the Five Pillars of Islam is to cleanse the self of desire, straighten the vital force, level the understanding of right and wrong, settle the heart's movements, and temper one's emotions and responses in the face of joy, anger, gain, and loss.

Chapter 6: The Virtues of Heart and Nature

Within the nature of man, there are five virtues: benevolence, righteousness, propriety, wisdom, and faith. These virtues guide one in acting justly within the world. Within the workings of the heart, there are five virtues as well: joy, anger, love, hatred, and desire. These reside within the self. And within the domain of knowledge, there are yet five more virtues: memory, retention, understanding, planning, and application. These virtues are employed in the world through action.

In each of these three realms, one must strive to maintain balance, for to lean too far in any one direction is to stray from the path. The Five Pillars of Islam serve to correct such imbalance and guide one back to the Way of moderation.

Chapter 7: The Balanced State and Distorted Change

Man is born from four elements and perfected by five. In the beginning of one's nature, semen is as water, blood is as earth, warmth as fire, and that which stirs all change is the Qi. When form is made complete, the breath of air and fire join to bring forth wood, while earth and water unite to give rise to metal. Wood nurtures growth and vitality, while metal bestows firmness and clarity. Within man, the water of the semen, the fire of warmth, and the earth that shapes the bones form five aspects of being, with Qi at their center, known as the Innate Wisdom of the Soul.

These five elements possess their own nature and virtue. The nature of fire is to ascend, and its virtue is loftiness and brilliance. The nature of water is to descend, and its virtue is humility. The nature of wood is to grow, and its virtue is simplicity and sincerity. The nature of metal is to be firm, and its virtue is steadfastness. The nature of earth is to enfold and nurture, and its virtue is stillness and obedience. Yet these virtues must be nourished by the Qi, for only then can each keep to its proper course and preserve the balance of moderation.

Should the breath fail to nourish them, what is balanced becomes unbalanced, and what is right is turned to wrong. Thus, loftiness and brilliance may become violence, and desire shall swell. Humility may turn to flattery, and impure thoughts arise. Steadfastness may harden into stubbornness, and rigidity shall grow. Simplicity may be clouded by ignorance, turning one dull and foolish. Stillness may transform into sluggishness, rendering one dull and slothful. Once the five natures are altered, selfish desires emerge, and from these, all evil things unfold. All this arises from the Qi being unfed, causing the path of balance to be forsaken.

The Five Pillars of Islam offer the means to nourish the Qi, restoring the five natures to their balanced course. These first seven chapters summarize the origins of the Five Pillars; the following twenty-five chapters will expound upon their principles, and the final thirty-one chapters will elucidate their deeper significance. Together, they form a sacred record, encompassing sixty-three chapters, inscribed as a testament to the age of the blessed Prophet

Chapter 8: The Rite of Remembrance

Remembrance is the turning of the heart toward the Lord (Allah). It is to reflect often within one's breast, to continually speak words of remembrance, to carve them deep into the heart, maintaining sincerity and reverence as one praises the Lord's majesty. In all words and deeds, one must preserve the harmony of the Way, guarding even the smallest action from straying from the path of righteousness. Never forget the remembrance of the heart, and let not the utterance of remembrance cease from your lips.

The scripture says: "In your rising and resting, in your slumber and in your meals, remember always.[4]" And it is also said: "To those who remember the Lord, the Lord also remembers them.[5]" By remembrance of the Lord, transgressions are wiped away, and by the Lord's remembrance, all anxieties are stilled. Be mindful of your actions, and the Lord shall be your guardian.

Chapter 9: The Law of Remembrance

The heart is like unto a mirror. When it turns toward one thing, it must of necessity turn away from another. That which it faces is either the law of Heaven (the natural order) or the desires of man. The heart's direction is ever shifting—when it turns toward the law of Heaven, the desires of man find no place within, but when it turns toward human desire, the law of Heaven vanishes from its sight. All judgments of good and evil, all discernment of

4. Based on Quran 3:191.
5. Quran 2:152.

right and wrong, arise from the heart's orientation.

This matter is both perilous and subtle, requiring reverence and the utmost care. A single righteous thought may bring a lifetime of blessing, but a single unrighteous thought may lead to a lifetime of sorrow. To revere and to act without restraining the heart is like holding back a torrent or taming a wild steed. This must always be kept in mind, and one must often reflect upon oneself.

As the holy prophet has said, "When the heart is clouded, it is as a mirror sullied with dirt. But by remembrance, it may be polished until it shines once more."

Chapter 10: The Meaning of Remembrance

Remembrance signifies that which is never forgotten, the unceasing memory of one's true source. It is the remembrance of the origin from which the body was born, the root of one's very nature, which lies in the essence of creation. This essence is the highest good, and in remembering it, evil is dispelled. It is supremely pure, and in remembering it, all impurity is cleansed. It is utterly true, and in remembering it, falsehood is banished.

When remembrance reaches its fullness, evil fades away, impurity is no more, and falsehood vanishes. In that moment, one returns to the original source. As the holy prophet has said: "Through remembrance, one transcends. By transcending the material and the self, one returns to a state of primal purity. This is the meaning of returning to the origin, of finding the end in the beginning."

Chapter 11: The Principle of Remembrance

Between man and the Lord (Allah) there lies no true separation. Yet it is commanded that one turn their remembrance toward the Lord, to reveal the very absence of such division. Man perceives his own self as an essential object, unaware that all things have been created by Allah. He sees the world as an illusion, not knowing that the truth behind the illusion is the Lord Himself. If one remembers only people or things, then one perceives only people and things, losing sight of the Lord.

But if one's heart is wholly turned to remembrance of the Lord, then all things and the self alike fade away, leaving only the essence (dhat) of Allah, deep and clear as a tranquil sea. As the scripture says: "The Lord is present with man, nearer than his own heart and life.[6]" And further, it is said: "In remembrance, there must be no divided heart; in reverence, no divided heart; in service, no divided heart. A 'divided heart' is to place another alongside the Lord, and this is the gravest betrayal."

Chapter 12: The Proof of Remembrance

To remember with conscious intent is to remember the Lord from a man's perspective. To remember unconsciously, without thought, is to remember the Lord as He desires When man remembers the Lord, it requires effort, bound by time and place. But when the Lord remembers Himself, there are no bounds of time or place; it is no longer an act of human remembrance. There is neither motion nor thought, and it surpasses any notion of remembrance.

If even a single thought or action does not align with the Way, then it remains constrained by time and place. Yet, "when one remembers the Lord as He desires", action and stillness alike transcend self; there is no separation, thought, or memory. In this state, one responds freely and fully to all things, and this is what it means for the Lord to remember Himself. Thus, it is said, "Remembrance holds no fixed form." One is called to remember even in stillness, and to forget not in action. In all encounters, be upright; in dealings with others, be true—this is remembrance.

As the scripture records: "Whether governing or laboring in the fields, or counting (and practicing medicine), in all things hold to the Way—this, too, is remembrance." And the holy prophet has said, "Without remembrance, all endeavors shall falter. Yet to remember without action—can this truly be called remembrance?"

6. Quran 50:16.

Chapter 13: The Rite of Worship

Worship is the turning of the body toward the Lord (Allah). Five times each day, at appointed hours, worship is performed: at dawn (Fajr), midday (Dhuhr), afternoon (Asr), evening (Maghrib), and night (Isha). The number of cycles in each worship is set: four for dawn, ten for midday, four for afternoon, five for evening, and nine for night.

There are four movements in worship: standing, bowing, prostrating, and kneeling. In standing, one stands straight and faces forward, hands clasped, feet together, and eyes fixed upon the ground. In bowing, the upper body inclines forward, the neck is lowered, the back is kept level, hands rest upon the knees, and the gaze is upon the feet. In prostrating, one lowers the body and head to the ground, pressing both nose and forehead to the earth, with elbows and abdomen raised, eyes fixed upon the tip of the nose. In kneeling, one sits quietly upon the heels, lowering the head and placing hands upon the knees, with eyes resting upon the chest. These movements combine to complete one cycle of worship, and through all cycles, the worship itself is fulfilled.

Certain rules guide worship: to perform ablution, to wear attire suitable for worship, to pray in a clean place, to observe the proper time, to face the correct direction (qibla, the direction of Mecca), and to hold the correct intention. Five times each day, this worship is carried out; once every seven days, the faithful gather for communal worship; and twice a year, grand gatherings are held.

For those of special devotion, there is a dawn prayer (Salat al-Duha), consisting of two cycles, and in the night, a special prayer (Tahajjud), for which no set number is prescribed. The scripture states: "O believers, observe the appointed times of worship with care[7]." Here, 'the middle' means to observe the times precisely. The holy prophet has said: "The line between righteousness and betrayal lies solely in worship. To forgo worship when the appointed time has come is to betray the faith."

Chapter 14: The Manner of Worship

Worship must be performed with reverence, and the heart must be devout. Worship that lacks reverence and devotion is as though no worship were offered at all. The time for worship must be observed with sincerity, and it must be carried out daily without fail. Through sincerity and unbroken practice, worship bears its fruit.

Worship is the command of the Divine. When the appointed time for worship arrives, the body must be present, for to delay and not attend at the proper time is to prioritize one's own convenience and to act arrogantly before the Lord. If the body is in the place of worship, then the heart must be there as well; to be bodily present but absent in spirit renders the worship empty and hollow. Those who are arrogant before the Lord are those who defy, and those who are empty of spirit are in error. Defiance leads to ruin, and error prevents one from reaching the path to Heaven.

Therefore, worship must be performed with a focused spirit and a devoted heart. Inwardly, one should be devout; outwardly, solemn. The mind should not wander, nor should one be distracted by their surroundings. One should refrain from scratching the head, shifting the feet, or making any noise. Should one fail in these respects, the worship must be repeated.

As the holy prophet has said: "When offering worship to the Lord (Allah), do so as though you see Him before you. Even if you do not see the Lord, know that He truly sees you."

Chapter 15: The Essence of Worship

Worship is a stairway to draw nearer to God (Allah), a path to return to the original source. Human life is a journey from the realm of reason (Li Shi) to the realm of form (Xiang Shi), tra-

7. Quran 2:238.

versing many boundaries along the way. At each boundary, the individual takes on material characteristics, drifting ever further from their primordial position. These layers are separated by numerous stages, with seven primary levels: energy, water, fire, earth, metal, wood, and living beings.

From reason springs energy, which possesses the qualities of motion and transformation. From energy arises fire, bearing the trait of illumination. From fire comes water, with its fluid nature. From water emerges earth, with its cohesive properties. From earth springs metal, with its solidity. From metal arises wood, imbued with the power of growth. From wood comes life, alive with the essence of activity. These forms (manifestations) sustain one another, and within them, myriad emotions take root.

Through movement, desire is born. Growth gives rise to life and death. Solidity leads to union and separation. Cohesion begets dispersion. Circulation transcends boundaries. Illumination produces light and shadow. Motion and transformation result in cycles of activity and stillness. Yet all these emotions are foreign to the true nature of humanity. Emotions obstruct one's essence, and the essence becomes shrouded by emotions, veering from reason and straying farther each day.

Worship transcends these emotional barriers, allowing one to return to their pure, primordial state. Once restored to this state, external distractions fall away, and the true essence shines forth. Standing symbolizes humanity, gazing upward to heaven and standing firm upon the earth. Bowing embodies the posture of birds and beasts, with their backs to the heavens and faces toward the earth. Prostration represents submission, mirroring the stillness of grass and trees rooted in the earth. Kneeling evokes the quietude of mountains, stones, and the solid ground beneath us. Ascending and descending reflect the interplay of water and fire. Movement and circulation signify the essence of energy. Transitioning from motion to stillness is a return to the original state of tranquility.

Through these symbolic actions, worship conveys profound meaning. By transcending each stage, the worshiper journeys back to their original source and draws closer to God. In this lies the true purpose of worship: a return to purity and an approach to the Divine.

Chapter 16: The Principle of Worship

All things in existence fall into one of two states: "Flow" and "Obstruction." Flow is the principle (the Way), while Obstruction is the form (the material manifestation). Those bound to the material cannot grasp the principle, but those who return to the principle gain insight into both the essence and the material. Yet this does not mean one must forsake the material to seek the principle. If one comprehends the principle, then what once seemed an obstacle becomes a passage; if one fails to grasp the principle, then even what appears clear becomes an impediment.

Man is a being where principle and form are gathered together as one whole. When one is daily ensnared by the material, there can be no return to the state of Flow. Not only the body, but also the heart and spirit become hindered from returning. Why is this? Because the spirit is subjugated to the body. But if one seeks the principle daily, the material cannot impede it; not only the spirit, but the body as well shall not be hindered. Why is this? Because the body becomes transcended by the spirit.

When the spirit is governed by the body, even what seems clear becomes an obstacle. But when the body is transcended by the spirit, obstacles themselves turn to passages. Worship is the artful means by which the body is transcended by the spirit, a wondrous state that transforms obstacles into pathways of Flow. Attaining this state, one no longer perceives life and death as merely life and death, but comes to understand the presence of that which lies beyond both. Likewise, one no longer sees desire as mere desire but grasps the existence of that which is beyond both desire and its absence.

Through this understanding, even if one cannot wholly escape life and death, one may yet transcend them; even if one does not leave desire entirely, one may still cut through it. The transformation of material form allows obstacles to become pathways once more. Thus, the scripture, in urging the people to worship, seeks to return all obstacles to the state of Flow.

Chapter 17: The Proof of Worship

Worship is the essence of submission to the Lord (Allah). Where there is no lack of obedience, there is no neglect in worship.

To be obedient to the Lord is, in truth, to offer Him worship. This obedience has two facets: outward submission to the Lord's commands, and inward submission to the Lord's essential virtues. When both the outward and the inward are aligned in obedience, both the outer and inner self are engaged in worship. And when obedience is continual, then worship is offered in all moments.

If the Lord commands me to remember, I remember; if He commands me to worship, I worship. For it is not the acts of remembrance or worship that hold virtue, but the obedience itself that is virtuous. Conversely, it is not the absence of remembrance or worship that constitutes error, but the lack of obedience.

True obedience is to follow the Lord's command precisely as it is given. The Lord has no fixed direction, so I am bound to no particular direction. The Lord has no form, so I am not ensnared by form. The Lord has neither sound, color, scent, nor taste, so I am not led astray by any of these. Holding to my true remembrance with a single-hearted devotion, I reach a place of serene tranquility, allowing all things to flow in their natural course.

If one is obedient but does not worship, obedience lacks its proper effect. And if one worships but is not obedient, such worship holds no virtue. To worship at the appointed times, with unceasing obedience—this is the mark of the true worshiper.

Chapter 18: The Rite of Fasting

Fasting is the expression of one's true nature in devotion to the Lord (Allah). Once each year, for one month, the fast is observed. Before dawn, one takes a meal, and after sunset, the fast is broken. During the day, no food or water touches the lips, no closeness to the opposite sex is permitted, and all mundane tasks are set aside. No distracting thoughts are entertained; the people do not gather in the marketplace, officials do not attend to cases, rulers do not hold court, and not to mention going on tour in countryside. Some remain within their households, while others retreat to temples, each reflecting upon themselves, purifying their faults, and turning solely to the Divine, casting aside all selfish desires.

The holy prophet has said, "Fasting is a virtue of restraint. By pausing one's labors and halting affairs of state, its profound significance is revealed."

Chapter 19: The Practice of Fasting

Fasting is a means of restraining desire, exercising caution in one's deeds, guarding body and mind with care, and avoiding reckless action. The eyes must not linger upon needless sights, the ears must not hear what is unseemly, the mouth must not speak in vain, the heart must not dwell on idle thoughts, the hands must not grasp and give what is unjust, and the feet must not tread upon forbidden paths. One must distance oneself from worldly desires, dedicating the heart solely to virtue and sincerity.

True fasting is not simply a matter of restraining desire or shunning wicked thoughts. To avoid wicked thoughts while neglecting to abstain from food breaks the divine command of fasting. Eating and carnal desire are the roots of all longing; to fail in restraining these is to fail in controlling desire. What meaning, then, can fasting hold for one who cannot control desire?

The holy prophet has said, "Fasting is not merely the abstinence from food and carnal desire, but the restraint of the ears, eyes, body, and heart in all things." He further said, "To possess desire is common to both man and beast; what sets man apart from beast is his ability to master that desire."

Chapter 20: The Meaning of Fasting

All deeds that stray from virtue are preceded by desire, with vitality and blood acting as their accomplices. By observing the fast, desire is subdued, vitality and blood are brought into harmony, and reckless actions are stilled. Virtue nourishes the heart, and from the heart, its influence spreads to the body. Conversely, food and drink nourish the body, yet they can weigh upon the heart. Fasting, by abstaining from food and drink, tempers one's temperament and fortifies the heart. When the heart is strong, clarity arises; with clarity, selfish desires fade, and the true nature emerges.

The holy prophet has said, "All things have their Zakat, and fasting is the trial that brings harmony to vitality and blood." The scripture says: "The Lord speaks to Prophet Isa 'In hunger, find enlightenment; in solitude, find unity.'" This means that, through abstinence, one's virtue is enriched, the true nature is revealed, and detachment from selfish attachments returns one to reverence, thus achieving a genuine oneness. The state in which not a speck of dust mars the spirit and no selfish intent remains is called "solitude (Gu)."

Chapter 21: The Principle of Fasting

Food, drink, and the desires of the flesh are necessary for survival and for the sustenance of life's journey; they are needs that cannot be avoided. Yet those who seek the Way reduce their reliance upon food and desire, while those who have attained the ideal forsake them entirely. This is because they regard food and desire as burdens and take delight in freedom from them.

Food and desire are needs acquired after birth, and to pursue them endlessly is to sink deeper into these acquired longings, gradually obscuring and separating oneself from the original essence. By restraining these acquired desires and allowing the inborn nature to shine forth, one recalls the primordial state and comes close to returning to it. And in returning to that primordial state, how close one draws to the original intent of the Lord (Allah).

Thus it is said, "Fasting belongs to the Lord, and the Lord shall bestow its reward." For this is a state of utmost closeness.

Chapter 22: The Proof of Fasting

To merely abstain from food and desire, yet be unable to forget them, is not true fasting. To refrain from wrongful acts, yet be unable to banish wrongful thoughts entirely, is not true fasting. To observe the fast but feel none of its effects—this too is not true fasting. Only those who no longer wish for food and desire, who almost forget their existence, who dread unworthy thoughts to the point of nearly forgetting them, and who shun worldly passions to find delight in the Heavenly Decree—these are the ones who reap the true benefits of fasting.

The holy prophet has said, "Fasting dissolves the temperament, much like the refining of gold, melting away impurities and gathering what is scattered." If, while fasting, one's temperament remains unpurified and one's heart is still scattered and unfocused, this is not true fasting. To distance oneself from food and desire is but the first step of fasting; to restrain desires and act with caution is the higher form. To conquer all selfish inclinations and wholly forget both the world and oneself—this is the ultimate form of fasting.

Thus, it is said, "Fasting is a withdrawal from the external, a severing of attachments, and a transformation of the self. To welcome nothing into the heart—this is the essence of true fasting."

Chapter 23: The Rite of Almsgiving

Almsgiving (Zakat) is the use of one's wealth in devotion to the Lord (Allah). The Lord has no need of wealth Himself; rather, to share it with the poor is to use it for His sake. Those who meet the prescribed threshold (Nisab) must give one-fortieth of their wealth. Gold, silver, currency, property, cattle, sheep, camels, horses, fruits, grains, and all forms of produce are governed by their own specific laws, calculated precisely and without concealment, and almsgiving is performed once each year.

Those who receive alms are the impoverished and those of noble character. One first aids those near, then those farther away; the remaining alms are submitted to the authorities, stored to relieve hunger and support education. One must not give to the unworthy, nor permit the unworthy to receive. Great care and consideration are required between the giver and the receiver.

The holy prophet has said, "All things have their due, and the capable are to assist those without. The wealthy aid the poor, the learned guide the ignorant, the eloquent resolve disputes, the strong support the weak. They build great houses to welcome guests, gather essential tools to lend as needed. All these acts embody the purpose of almsgiving."

Chapter 24: The Practice of Almsgiving

To possess much and yet share it freely, to temper one's own desires and find joy in giving to others—this is the way of the virtuous. Even the smallest trace of concealment can undermine all good deeds. When giving for the sake of truth, one must give with joy, neither imposing obligation nor seeking honor. To give with selfish intent is as flawed as concealing with selfish intent.

Gifts born of labor or acts of charity stemming from chivalry do not fulfill the merit of almsgiving (Zakat) and do not fall within its requirements. One must exercise utmost care in choosing a worthy recipient and, likewise, accept only after careful consideration of whether the gift is rightly deserved. To give without due thought is the error of the giver, while to accept without clarity is the error of the receiver.

Chapter 25: The Meaning of Almsgiving

Almsgiving (Zakat) is the great law that embodies the will of the Lord, that teaches love for others, the forgetting of self, and the letting go of material things. The Most High (Allah) is the source of boundless mercy, giving freely and generously. Our acts of charity are nothing less than reflections of His mercy. To regard all people as part of one's own body, to love them as oneself, and to share in their well-being—this is to love others as one loves oneself.

To release one's possessions is to forget them; to be unbound by things is to be free from their hold. Humanity, often cherishing itself too greatly, does not easily give rise to the virtues of compassion and justice. Yet through the practice of Zakat, one attains the four virtues: compassion, self-forgetfulness, detachment from material things, and justice.

Chapter 26: The Principle of Almsgiving

What one truly possesses from birth is virtue alone. All external things serve merely as tools to cultivate virtue, the body itself included. If these tools, meant to foster virtue, instead bring harm, they cease to be tools and become burdens. Not only do external possessions weigh upon the spirit, but the body itself may also become a burden.

The noble are not ensnared by such burdens; they regard even body and life as not truly their own. Those of middling character understand the weight of such burdens and can set them aside, while those of lesser understanding cling to them, unaware of their load until the end. The law of Zakat teaches one to relinquish attachment to external things and to let one's inherent virtues shine forth.

Chapter 27: The Proof of Almsgiving

The purpose of offering Zakat is to free oneself from attachment to selfish desires. If one still clings to wealth or harbors self-centered attachments, then Zakat holds no meaning. Yet, it is not required that one surrender all possessions; rather, one must give without reluctance, without resentment, and with joy, regardless of the amount requested. When wealth is asked, one gives wealth; when strength is needed, one gives strength. Such a person aids others as they would ease their own suffering, without distinction between self and others.

One should view the acquisition of wealth as a temporary stewardship, and its loss as a natural return. What remains should be seen as burden and peril, not as a source of happiness or virtue. If one feels as though crossing a treacherous path burdened with weight and longs to set it down, then one's heart is rightly placed.

The common man's attachment lies in wealth, while the noble soul's attachment lies in the self. If there remains any clinging in the heart, any attachment to self, true Zakat has not yet been achieved. Only those who have let go of body, possessions, and worldly gain—seeking neither reward nor favor—are the ones who practice Zakat in its truest sense.

Chapter 28: The Rite of Pilgrimage

The pilgrim, in undertaking the Hajj, offers body, heart, and wealth entirely to the Lord, seeking to return to the primordial state of unity with the Divine. Mecca is the place of humankind's creation, the cradle of origin. In the appointed month, the pilgrim embarks on the sacred journey, reaching the stations of pilgrimage, there receiving the sacred ordinances, purifying in ritual bath, and donning simple garments. Adornments are set aside, no animal is slaughtered, and One must perform the Hajj first as soon as he arrives at the Ka'abah.

One feeds his beasts of burden and sacrificial animals on the 7th day of Dhul-Hijjah Month, and on the morrow, a great gathering is held at Mina, a plain south of Mecca, where all assemble without distinction of rank or station. In the morning, they stand upon Mount Arafat; by evening, they journey to Muzdalifah. With the dawn, they return to Mina, where the great ritual of casting stones is held. With this, the ordinances are lifted, an animal is sacrificed, and the pilgrim bathes, dons ceremonial attire, and anoints with fragrant incense.

Then they enter the Kaaba, touching the Black Stone and

circumambulating the House seven times. In designated places (Maqām Ibrāhīm), they bow in prayer, offering their supplications, climbing Mount Safa, facing the Kaaba, and lifting prayers to the heavens. Words of praise are chanted, songs of worship sung, and prayers offered.

Afterward, they traverse the plain of white earth, performing the ritual journey between the two hills of Safa and Marwah. Returning once more to the Kaaba, they continue their pilgrimage in accordance with the rites and then return to Mina. The next day, they cast stones again, completing the ritual on the following day. The pilgrim then visits the Prophet's tomb, seeks out the sacred spring, and, having completed the holy rites, returns homeward.

Chapter 29: The Practice of Pilgrimage

The pilgrimage (Hajj) is the summation of the Five Pillars, the great gathering of Heaven and man. The heart remains unceasing in its faith, and words of prayer do not leave the lips. In worship, one advances carefully, step by step, meeting the Divine with utmost reverence. In fasting, one refrains from outward actions and restrains inner thoughts, keeping body and soul in a state of stillness. Without relying on wealth or diminishing sincerity, one devotes all that one possesses to the journey.

The pilgrim leaves home and ventures forth, moving from the familiar to the distant, severing attachments, forsaking one's homeland, and traversing difficult roads. Among all acts of devotion, none demands so much effort or endurance as this. Though love is shown, one must guard against loving oneself excessively. It is not for the purpose of seeing or learning, it should not be regarded as separation from one's family and homeland, nor is one's arrival alone considered the fulfillment of virtue. Rather, the strict observance of ordinances, meticulous attention to each step, and the precision of both inner and outer conduct are paramount, embodying the virtues of sincerity and devotion.

Chapter 30: The Meaning of Pilgrimage

When a person's love for their homeland grows too deep, their yearning for truth wanes. The pilgrim embarks on a journey to distant lands, severing attachments, drawing nearer to the primordial source. By leaving behind the familiar and undertaking a difficult path, the pilgrim reaches the sacred grounds. This journey is akin to the seeker's path, wherein one overcomes selfish desires, enduring toil and discipline to return to truth.

Through the physical journey of pilgrimage, the soul is awakened to the inner journey. The finest of pilgrims turn not only their bodies but their hearts toward the Divine, distancing themselves from the land of selfish desire, transcending the bounds of attachment and aversion, reaching the gates of reverence and justice. They perform the purifying ablution, casting aside the garments of human desire, donning the ordinances of Heavenly law, ascending the mount of wisdom, and gathering on the outskirts of perpetual peace.

Having sacrificed the desires of body and spirit, they enter the sacred sanctuary, touch the Black Stone shrouded in mystery, and worship at the threshold of Divine covenant, becoming one with the the Kaaba of Unity with Lord. Outwardly, the traces of the pilgrimage remain, yet inwardly, they are united with the Divine essence. Can any other attainment surpass such a journey?

As the scripture says, "Abandon thyself and come to this place." This is the true meaning of pilgrimage: to relinquish selfishness and to follow the eternal law of Heaven.

Chapter 31: The Principle of Pilgrimage

The essence of pilgrimage (Hajj) lies in its meaning: "to return." To return is the deepest longing of humankind, the natural inclination of all living things. When a traveler returns home, when a messenger completes their mission and comes back, these are acts of return. The bird returns to its forest, the fish to the deep waters, and all rivers flow into the sea—all these are returns. To "return" is rooted in the inherent nature of all things; it is not something forced or achieved through effort. To prevent one who wishes to return is a violation of nature itself, just as one who returns but finds no rest at their destination finds no peace.

However, whenever one is away, it is for a purpose, and until that purpose is fulfilled, one cannot truly "return." Our time in this world is like a traveler's sojourn at an inn, for one day we shall surely return. Yet, there are duties to fulfill before that return can be realized. Only once these duties are complete can one truly return.

The prophets, having fulfilled their divine duties, returned, yet they looked with compassion upon those who could not find their way back, and established the law to guide them. The wise follow this law, leading others along the path of return; the learned also follow and find their way home. But the foolish do not seek to return; they cling to their desires, becoming so lost that they forget the way home and, in the end, know not how to return.

The pilgrimage reminds us of the place to which we must return and urges us toward it. Return is natural; why should it require effort? The noble return without effort; those of middling character return with great exertion. But the foolish, even with effort, do not return. Thus, the foolish remain bound by their ignorance, and in the end, they fall below even the beasts.

Chapter 32: The Proof of Pilgrimage

The relationship between Truth (the cosmic order) and humankind is akin to that between the Kaaba in Mecca, the sacred courtyard where pilgrims gather during the Hajj, and all under Heaven. The Kaaba stands open and accessible to all who would come; yet, if one turns away, each day they drift farther, and even should they face toward it, without complete dedication to the path, they cannot reach it. The Kaaba itself places no obstacle before any person, yet people hinder themselves. Similarly, Truth presents no barrier to humankind; it is people who distance themselves from it.

Truth lies near to all, pervading every place, yet it is the manner and degree of one's striving that distinguish sage from commoner, wise from foolish. Truth, in its essence, flows unbound, but it is man who raises barriers; Truth is inherently clear, but it is man who obscures it. If one were to one day turn inward and face Truth with sincerity, the distinctions of sage, commoner, wise, and foolish would fall away.

The Kaaba has distance and a set place, yet Truth is beyond direction or measure. The pilgrimage of the appointed month is but an outward form of this journey to the Kaaba; in turning one's self sincerely to Truth, one enters the pilgrimage at all times and places. When one lives in perpetual pilgrimage, all thoughts arise from the Divine, and every deed follows the command of the Lord. Remembrance, prayer, fasting, and almsgiving—all find their fulfillment in a single pilgrimage. Body and mind, nature and life, can be perfected through this one pilgrimage. Loyalty, honor, and integrity are likewise completed within it; all that lies within the Heavenly Way and the human path are encompassed in the single act of pilgrimage. Thus, it is said that "Pilgrimage is the gathering of all Five Pillars."

Yet should there be the slightest thought or deed within one's heart that diverges from Truth, it constitutes a departure from Truth and negates the essence of pilgrimage. Thus, to observe a person's pilgrimage, it is enough to consider their daily practice and their manner in the smallest of acts.

Chapter 33: The Five Devotions

What is the habit of remembrance of Allah according to time? It is the discipline of the heart. The heart knows no stillness, and likewise, thought is ever in motion. Within the subtle movements of the heart dwell the seeds of reason and desire, the roots of good and evil. A single misstep, even for a fleeting moment, may cast a shadow upon one's entire life.

By practicing remembrance at each appointed time, one guards against this, controlling the heart and keeping it from heedlessness.

What, then, are the five daily times of prayer? Prayer is the discipline of the body. The body, engaged in many activities, should pray in moments of rest.

At dawn, before any work or labor has begun, when time is yet unburdened, one should offer the morning prayer. In the afternoon, when the day's toil reaches a pause and the body is at ease, one should offer prayer. At midday, when all tasks have been laid to rest and there is ample time, one should offer prayer. In the evening, when all duties are complete and one returns to the home, one should offer prayer.

And at night, when all creation settles into slumber, bringing rest to both body and heart, one should offer prayer.

If one forsakes prayer at these times, prioritizing one's own convenience, it is defiance of the Divine command—a self-centered act.

The five daily prayers represent five central points in the day's journey. The morning prayer marks the transition from night to day, the evening prayer from day to night; noon prayer is the heart of the day, night prayer the anchor of the night, and afternoon prayer the pivot among these times.

The scripture says, "Guard well the center of your prayers[8]," and this is its meaning.

The sages of old began prayer at these five times, preserving their teaching to this day, following in the path of saints long past.

What, then, is the purpose of fasting one month each year? Fasting is the discipline of one's nature. Though one's original nature is pure and free from effort, the life of humankind is bound to many tasks. Duties to family and state, labor in fields and trade, call for ceaseless endeavor; thus, for one month each year, people fast, pausing from work and halting affairs of state. This grants rest to the people, avoiding undue hardship.

What of almsgiving (Zakat), once a year? It is the discipline of one's wealth.

Throughout the seasons, crops grow, trade flows, and accounts settle. Then, by giving a fixed portion, one's essential wealth remains whole.

Why give one-fortieth? It is said that all creation is completed at forty, and so a portion is taken from abundance to be given to those in need.

And what of the pilgrimage, once in a lifetime? It is the discipline of offering body, heart, and wealth, leaving behind homeland and kin.

This journey is arduous for many, and thus once in a lifetime is sufficient.

If one cannot make the pilgrimage, a journey within one's own land may suffice. The great pilgrimage once a year and the minor pilgrimage once every seven days show that the teachings of the saints, though ardent, are never forced.

8. Quran 2:238.

Chapter 34: The Gatherings

When people gather together in worship, it is called "the Assembly," while the prayer observed once every seven days is called "the Gathering" (Jumu'ah), and the prayer held twice a year is called "the Festival." There are five prayers each day, a Gathering once a week, and Festivals twice a year.

The Festival signifies all gatherings; the Gathering signifies all acts of worship; and the Assembly signifies the union of all people. The word "Festival" thus represents the bringing together of all gatherings, a symbol of unity across the world. The Festival unites the Gatherings, the Gatherings unify the Assemblies, the Assemblies unify the People, the People unify the Body, the Body unifies the Spirit, and the Spirit unifies the Heart. This is called the "Assembly of the Soul," and it is greater than the "Assembly of Forms."

The Assembly of Forms occurs in time, but the Assembly of the Principle transcends time. Thus, a person of wisdom may experience both Assemblies in a single breath.

Chapter 35: The Counsel of Worship

Why should worship be performed in congregation? People are often consumed by the duties of daily life, their hearts weighed down with myriad thoughts. Thus, even when they stand in prayer, they carry anxieties within. Yet, by entering the sacred space of the Masjid and worshipping alongside others, they come to act with humility and reverence, subdued by the solemnity of the holy place. Within the ordered ranks and solemn atmosphere, any trace of indolence fades, and a spirit of sincerity and devotion arises.

It is in this manner that the true blessings of worship are attained. The holy prophet has said, "Congregational prayer holds seventy times the merit of individual prayer." Thus, it is also said, "Those who dwell near the Masjid should not pray at home but should pray in the Masjid"

Why is there a Gathering (Jumu'ah) once every seven days? The number seven symbolizes Heaven and Earth. By observing worship every seven days and forming a complete cycle of worship, we reflect the order of the cosmos.

And why are there two Festivals each year? The Festival signifies the unity to which all things ultimately return. The two annual Festivals are each of a distinct nature: one, the "Festival of Opening," signifies the fulfillment of the Heavenly Way, while the other, the "Festival of Sacrifice," signifies the completion of the human path.

Chapter 36: The Measure of Worship

The Great Worship is composed of both rituals and their deeper meaning. It aligns with the laws of the seven heavens, forming a complete rite of worship. There are twelve Fard conditions and twelve Wajib conditions ordained by the Almighty; the number of Sunna conditions is twenty-eight, embodying the eternal wheel of the heavens and encompassing the cycles of the sun and moon. It holds the profound significance of the Five Elements and summarizes all the labors of creation. This is the rite of worship.

In worship, one washes away one's sins, prays for the peace of the ruler, remembers the grace of one's parents, and gives thanks for the teachings of one's mentors. One cherishes the bonds of friendship and prays for the well-being of all living creatures. This is the true meaning of worship.

The acts of worship are numbered: within each day, there are thirty-two bows, sixty-four prostrations with the forehead to the ground, one hundred seventy-eight praises (Takbirat), twelve gestures of uplifted hands, seventeen instances of kneeling, thirty-two risings, twenty-seven standings, eleven turns to the right and left, five adhan, and five iqamah. Altogether, these acts amount to three hundred eighty-four in a day. This number aligns with the foundations of creation and the laws governing the division of day and night.

Chapter 37: The Symbols of Worship

The act of bowing one's forehead to the ground symbolizes the way that grass and trees root themselves deep into the earth. The bowing of the body is an image of birds and beasts who bear the heavens upon their backs as they move through life. The posture of kneeling represents the mountains and hills, steadfast and firmly seated upon the earth. To stand upright symbolizes humankind, who rises beneath the sky and walks upon the land. The turning and rising motions reflect the shifting of Yin and Yang and the eternal course of the sun and moon.

Thus, worship embraces all elements of Heaven and Earth.

Chapter 38: The Origins of Worship

The first to offer the morning prayer (Fajr) was Adam. The first to perform the midday prayer (Dhuhr) was Ibrahim (Abraham). The first to observe the afternoon prayer ('Asr) was Yunus (Jonah). The first to conduct the evening prayer (Maghrib) was 'Isa (Jesus). The first to offer the night prayer ('Isha) was Musa (Moses). And the first to perform the Witr, the special prayer of the night, was the Prophet Muhammad.

The prophets of old each established their own prayers, but it was our Prophet Muhammad who gathered them all and perfected them. Thus, it is said, "The Way is made complete, virtue is fulfilled, and it stands as a marvel throughout the ages."

Chapter 39: Sincerity of Heart

What becomes of acts performed without sincerity? To offer prayer without earnestness, to attend worship without reverence, to give alms without joy, to fast without reflection, or to undertake pilgrimage without meticulous care—what, then, are these acts?

If prayer is not sincere, it is as though no prayer were offered. If worship is not approached with reverence, it is as though worship never occurred. If almsgiving is done without joy, it is as though no alms were given. If fasting is not accompanied by self-reflection, it is as though one had never fasted. If pilgrimage is not fulfilled with precision, it is as though one had never journeyed.

The shaykh (master) has said, "All deeds are rooted in the heart and are perfected by intention." Thus, When a simple-minded man longs for the sands to be transformed into grains with the help of Lord, his intention would be recorded as a good act due to his sincerity; On the contrary, even a Sheikh could go astray for the slightest suspicion of Lord's power, even though he has practiced various 'ibadah over one hundred years. How, then, can those who seek the Way not treat their hearts and intentions with utmost care?

Chapter 40: The Five Symbols

Worship embodies the symbols of all creation. Fasting imitates the stance of the Lord, who observes but does not partake. Almsgiving (Zakat) mirrors the heavens and earth, which bestow their blessings without taking in return. Pilgrimage reflects the rivers, which all flow back to their source. Remembrance (Dhikr) holds no fixed form, allowing it to reach the profound depths of stillness.

Thus, among the Five Pillars, remembrance is the most essential and the greatest of all. It stands as the central axis upon which all deeds revolve.

Chapter 41: The Gates of Virtue

The Five Pillars of Islam are the gateway into virtue, the stairway ascending to Heaven, the path of subtlety, and the essence of all creation. They serve as a sieve to filter selfish desires, a forge to refine one's character, a fountain to cleanse away faults, and a ship to cross the vast sea. In cultivating and nurturing both body and spirit, none who follow this path will fail to find success.

Chapter 42: Drought and Rain

The Five Pillars of Islam stand as rain amidst drought, a spring in times of thirst, a lantern in the darkest night, a bridge over turbulent rivers, a cloud under the blazing sun, and a balm to heal the ailments of life. Throughout the ages, whenever humanity has faced hardship, there has been none who sought solace in the Five Pillars and remained without relief. They are not merely acts of devotion but enduring sources of sustenance, guiding the faithful through the trials of existence and illuminating the path toward divine peace.

Chapter 43 : The Five Blessings

Remembrance honors the Lord, worship strikes down the adversary, fasting quenches the flames of desire, almsgiving soothes calamity, and pilgrimage severs all worldly bonds.

Chapter 44: The Five Breaths

Within the Five Pillars of Islam lies a path of ceaseless circulation. Each serves as the beginning for the others and as their end, each embodies their essence and enacts their purpose. They are each the outer form and the inner truth, complementing one another, and thus continue in an unending cycle.

Chapter 45: The Transformations

The Five Pillars of Islam govern the five senses (sight, hearing, smell, speech, and touch), express the five virtues (benevolence, righteousness, propriety, wisdom, and faithfulness), and fulfill the five constants of moral conduct. They honor the Five Elements (wood, fire, earth, metal, and water) and bring completeness to the five fundamental principles of social order. Moreover, the Five Pillars participate in the creation and nurturing of Heaven and Earth, harmonizing with the laws of Yin and Yang.

Chapter 46: Unceasing Practice

The perfected one, the sage of the highest path, embodies the Five Pillars in unbroken continuity. Such a one engages in remembrance of the Divine without conscious effort, worships without bending the body or bowing the head, fasts without renouncing food or desire, gives alms without distributing wealth or grain, and performs pilgrimage without facing a specific direction. This is the great form of the Five Pillars.

But can ordinary people follow such a path? A careful reading of this chapter reveals that the perfected one's sincerity and reverence are already so deeply rooted that they fulfill these practices continuously, without interruption. Thus, it is called "unceasing" and does not mean that they forgo the Five Pillars. Readers should proceed with care in understanding this. Without careful thought and deep insight, there is a danger of misinterpretation, a misstep that is by no means trivial. There is a fear that those who interpret this rashly or without care may use it to support misguided arguments, harming both themselves and others. Alas, this is indeed a sorrowful matter.

Yet those who attain this higher state of inner cultivation are at one with the Five Pillars, while still upholding the outward forms. Indeed, it is said that the prophets and wise ones of old never abandoned the outward practices of the Five Pillars. Thus, let the reader take heed, with utmost caution—be careful, and careful again!

Chapter 47: The Whole Body

The Five Pillars of Islam permeate the entire being, leaving nothing untouched. Among the Five Pillars, there are those performed with the heart, those enacted by the body, those fulfilled by the hands and feet, those realized by the head, and those engaged by the ears, eyes, mouth, and nose. Each part of the body is susceptible to its own failings, and for every failing, there exists a corresponding act of purification. The Five Pillars are the integration of all these acts, a unity encompassing every aspect of one's being.

Chapter 48: Belonging and Intent

Remembrance (Dhikr) belongs to the heart, and the heart is of the finest subtlety. Its expression lies in words spoken from the mouth, representing benevolence in character and filial piety in human virtues. Among the Five Elements, it corresponds to fire.

Worship (Salat) belongs to the body, the source of movement. Its practice is manifested through bodily actions, signifying propriety in character and brotherly love in human virtues. In the Five Elements, it corresponds to earth.

Fasting (Sawm) belongs to the will, and will to the breath. Through fasting, one guards against the sights of the eyes and carefully restrains the thoughts of the heart. It embodies wisdom in character and temperance in human virtues. Among the Five Elements, it corresponds to wood.

Almsgiving (Zakat) belongs to knowledge, and knowledge to blood. Proper giving involves keen listening, signifying righteousness in character and friendship in human virtues. In the Five Elements, it corresponds to water.

Pilgrimage (Hajj) belongs to one's essence, and essence to life itself. Pilgrimage completes all actions and influences all things, rendering the nose indifferent even to fragrance. It represents faithfulness in character and loyalty in human virtues. Among the Five Elements, it corresponds to metal.

Chapter 49: Forgetfulness and Aspiration

When remembrance reaches a state of selflessness, one becomes a true rememberer. When worship reaches a state of self-forgetfulness, one becomes a true worshipper. When fasting reaches a realm free of desire for food or pleasures, one becomes a true faster. When almsgiving is performed without attachment to wealth, one becomes a true giver. When pilgrimage transcends physical movement and direction, one becomes a true pilgrim.

Thus, when remembrance is not confined to the heart, the whole being becomes an act of remembrance. When worship is not limited to the body, all actions become worship. When fasting is not limited to abstaining from food or desire, detachment itself becomes fasting. When almsgiving is not bound to wealth, the absence of self-interest becomes almsgiving. When pilgrimage is not restricted to physical travel, every place becomes pilgrimage.

If one can attain this state, the five senses will open, the five virtues will shine forth, the five vital energies will align, and the five endeavors will find fulfillment.

Chapter 50: The Opening of the Senses

Remembrance opens the mouth, worship purifies the body, fasting opens the eyes, almsgiving opens the ears, and pilgrimage opens the nose. Thus, with a single act of remembrance, Adam opened the heavens and earth; Luqman gained subtle wisdom through continuous remembrance; and Musa, after forty days of devotion, spoke with the Divine. The Prophet Muhammad, with a single sigh, stirred the heavens and brought forth wondrous souls.

By renewing worship, Adam was freed from hardship, and Khidr gained long life through diligent prayer. 'Isa (Jesus), through his daily worship, ascended bodily to the heavens. The Prophet Muhammad never neglected his prayers due to his public affairs; thus, his whole being became light, casting no shadow beneath the sun, no fly landing upon his garments, and he walked above the ninth heaven.

Through fasting, Ibrahim perceived the subtleties of truth, and Musa beheld the Divine in his hunger. The Prophet Muhammad discerned circumstances beneath graves, understood the essence of all creation, comprehended the beginning and end of the heavens and earth as if they lay in his palm, and gazed directly upon the Divine presence beyond human understanding.

Through his noble almsgiving, Hatim al-Ta'i heard the cries of the hungry from a hundred miles away, Sulaiman never hesitated to bring relief to others, thus he was given by Lord the gift of understanding animals' languages. The Prophet Muhammad heard the footsteps of angels in the ninth heaven, received warning from a sheep of impending danger, perceived the innocence in a woman's plea, and received Divine revelation daily.

Through his devotion, Yaqub detected the scent of Yusuf's robe from a thousand miles away, his heart wholly focused upon him. So too did the Prophet Muhammad at times sense the fragrance of the blessed realms and discern scent within what is unscented.

The nose is a gateway to the heavens, while the mouth is an entryway to the earth. Through the nose, the breath flows, and through the mouth, the breath is renewed in constant rhythm. The Five Pillars are all wondrous, with both essence and symbol in perfect harmony, without hindrance or obstruction.

Chapter 51: The Effects of Devotion

Through remembrance, one contemplates the Lord in stillness, awaiting the movements of the world. In this way, all external motion is drawn inward. Through worship, one acts with intention, experiencing the stillness of the world. Thus, all external calmness expands within.

In fasting, when one attains a state of desirelessness, the heart is no longer troubled by cravings, and love and aversion become balanced. In almsgiving, when self-interest is forsaken, selfish desires no longer weigh upon one's soul, and gain and loss are held equally. Pilgrimage is a return to one's original state; by perfecting reason and fulfilling one's true nature, one ultimately arrives at the essence of life. Heaven and humankind become perfectly attuned, and all that was once obstructed now flows freely.

As a result, one hears all without the need to listen, sees all without the need to look, speaks without words, and moves without motion. In this state, one feels all and is connected to all. Afterward, understanding arises without thought, and accomplishment flows effortlessly. Knowledge encompasses all things, and the will of the Divine knows no bounds, so that every secret of Heaven and Earth rests within oneself.

At this point, Heaven employs humankind, and humankind employs Heaven. The harmony between the celestial and human realms is complete, revealing the original nature of the Heavenly Way. The vastness of Heaven and Earth is beyond measure; nothing rivals the brilliance of sun and moon, no spirit can comprehend these acts, and no calculation can record their merit. This is the effect of the Five Pillars.

The holy prophet has said, "To reach the utmost is to reach the Divine." Through the cultivation of the Pillars, Heaven and Earth are drawn into harmony—this is what it means for all creation to return to the Lord.

Chapter 52: The Three Ultimates

In Heaven, there are five stars; on Earth, there are the Five Elements—wood, fire, earth, metal, and water; within humankind, there are the five senses—hearing, sight, speech, smell, and movement; and within the soul, there are five virtues—benevolence, righteousness, propriety, wisdom, and faithfulness. To fulfill the way of humankind, there are the five principles of conduct, and to fulfill the way of Heaven, there are the Five Pillars of Islam.

These Five Pillars encompass all matters concerning Heaven, Earth, and humankind. If one desires to complete the Three Ultimates—Heaven, Earth, and Humankind—one may achieve this by following the practices and rituals of the Five Pillars, which bring all into harmony.

Chapter 53: The Symbols of Law

The principles of the Five Pillars are visible in the workings of Yin and Yang, and their essence fills Heaven and Earth. The practices of the Five Pillars manifest in the human body, for the human form itself is a grand assembly of Yin and Yang, Heaven and Earth. To seek Yin and Yang or Heaven and Earth apart from the human body is folly, for humanity embodies the symbols of the cosmos, fulfills the workings of Yin and Yang, and reflects the phenomena of Heaven and Earth.

If one speaks of the growth of plants, it is reflected in the growth and standing of the human body. The movements of birds and beasts mirror human walking and perception. The mysteries of the divine are seen in human wisdom and understanding. When we speak of Heaven's shelter and Earth's support, we refer to the human body and soul; the transformations of Yin and Yang and the turning of the seasons are reflected in human breath, growth, aging, and life's waxing and waning.

The breath of humankind is like wind and cloud; body warmth like the heat of fire. The nose rises like a mountain, and the mouth dips like a valley. Blood flows as rivers, muscles are as soft as earth, and bones as firm as stone. The laws of Heaven and Earth are all contained within humankind, and the symbols of Heaven and Earth are all visible within us.

Chapter 54: The Constant Virtue

The Five Pillars of Islam are the means by which the virtues of one's essence and life are brought to fulfillment. They complete the bond of righteousness between heaven and humanity, perfectly embodying the path of justice (al-'adl). The Five Pillars represent the universal obligations that every human being must perform, encompassing the constant and unchanging principles of existence.

Their significance is profound, and their essence is deeply enriching. Yet, though humanity dwells within them each day, few are truly aware of their presence or their profound importance.

Chapter 55: The Role and Power of the Five Pillars

The role of the Five Pillars is of profound magnitude, bridging the hidden mysteries of Heaven and humankind. Through them, one comes to understand both the unseen and the evident, reaching the subtle depths of one's true essence and comprehending the meaning of life and death. From afar, they flow like sacred waters, boundless and expansive, never diluted by the shallow or empty. In the near, they permeate daily actions, making their tangible impact all the more evident.

Their vastness knows no boundaries, and their fineness no gaps. They cycle with the passage of time, and across all ages remain ever steadfast.

Chapter 56: The Universal Principle

The Five Pillars serve as the path for cultivating the self. Their law encompasses Heaven and Earth, leaving nothing outside its reach. Their teachings embrace both the sage and the common soul, allowing none to escape its embrace. From the young to the old, men and women alike, all are bound by its principles without exception.

Its rites and rituals embody the vastness of Heaven and Earth, symbolizing all creation, encompassing even the divine. Performed with quiet reverence, they require strength tempered by solemn humility.

Chapter 57: The Sacred Law

The Five Pillars stand as an unchanging law throughout the ages, the model set by saints of old and the standard for saints to come. Commanded by the Lord and conveyed by the prophets, they are taught to humankind, who follow their path. In embodying the Lord's will and taking the saints as their example, the Five Pillars manifest the virtues of the holy. Junayd used to say through his complete practice of the Five Pillars, the holy prophet become a beacon for all generations.

Chapter 58: The Ladder of Law

The prophets established teachings as a ladder, enabling humankind to ascend toward Heaven. The station of Heaven is high and distant, and thus, the ladder is composed of many steps—none can reach it in a single stride.

Remembrance (Dhikr) expresses the desire to ascend to Heaven. Worship (Salat) is the method of ascent. Almsgiving (Zakat) severs the pull of worldly desires. Fasting (Sawm) allows one to forget the self. When one has severed worldly attachment and transcended the self, one attains Heaven. And in reaching Heaven, one grasps the true essence of pilgrimage.

Chapter 59: Simplicity and Depth

The path of the prophets appears shallow yet runs deep; it seems near yet stretches far. The way that the prophets have shown is simple, their teachings sincere and compassionate. Yet why is it that people struggle to fully walk this path?

Though the prophets present it plainly, people perceive it as complex; though they offer it with ease, people find it difficult. When one sees complexity, one feels burdened; when one senses difficulty, one grows weary. In such a state of suffering and fatigue, how can one progress upon the path?

Thus, there are those who abandon the journey midway, and those who pledge to uphold the teachings but cannot fulfill them to the end.

Chapter 60: Position and Nurture

Heaven shields, Earth sustains, the sun and moon illuminate, the seasons cycle, rains and dews fall in their time, grass and trees sprout in their time, birds and beasts flourish in their time, and all things grow in their due season. All of this serves to nurture the Way, the will of the Lord.

Though humankind daily enjoys these blessings, those who do not dedicate themselves to the path forsake the Creator's intent. By striving in accordance with the Heavenly Way and fulfilling human virtues, one realizes the purpose of humanity's position and the work of nurturing creation.

Chapter 61: The Sacred and the Common

The Five Pillars of Islam serve as the measure by which humankind is observed. Whether prophet, sage, scholar, or fool, none can transcend the Five Pillars, for it is by them that the path of humanity is established.

A saint is deemed a saint because they practice the Five Pillars to perfection. A sage is deemed a sage because they follow the Five Pillars as their model. A scholar is deemed a scholar because they understand the principles of the Five Pillars. A fool is deemed a fool because they do not grasp these principles.

Those who are ignorant of the Five Pillars do not comprehend their essence nor attain their purpose. This can be likened to the act of eating and drinking: the saint is one who discerns and refines the taste, teaching others. The sage knows the taste and partakes of it. The scholar eats and comes to know the taste. The fool neither knows the taste nor partakes of it; even if they force themselves to eat, they ultimately fail to understand its flavor.

Chapter 62: Loyalty and Filial Piety

The Five Pillars of Islam serve as a daily standard by which people are measured. To serve one's parents without fulfilling the Five Pillars is not true filial piety. To serve one's ruler without reverence for the Five Pillars is not true loyalty. To live in the bonds of marriage or brotherhood without practicing the Five Pillars is not the way of righteousness. To interact with friends and neighbors without taking the Five Pillars as one's guide is to stray from the path.

If one listens with the ears, sees with the eyes, speaks with the mouth, scents with the nose, grasps with the hands, walks with the feet, thinks, and contemplates—yet does not practice the Five Pillars—then one deviates from proper conduct.

Thus, the perfected individual observes the Five Pillars without ceasing, neither resting day by day nor taking pause.

Chapter 63: Tawhid

The nature of the petty and the noble, the sage and the commoner, is essentially the same. It is only the shrouding of reason by desire, and the divergence of habits, that create the vast differences in human character. The Five Pillars of Islam unify reason and harmonize one's inner nature. They are a divine gift, like a marketplace where sages and common folk may gather alike.

The effect of remembrance (Dhikr) is to keep one free of conflicting thoughts; the noble Bayazid Bistami never questioned his disciples' names, focusing only on their virtue. Worship (Salat) enables one to remain unshaken by praise or criticism—just as, even when one struck the blessed tooth of the Prophet Muhammad, he maintained a noble disposition in adversity. Fasting (Sawm) empowers one to abandon desire and adapt to any situation; the wise Ibn Ata, after a bandit slew his nine children, uttered not a word.

The effect of almsgiving (Zakat) is a complete absence of self-interest; the Prophet Muhammad himself once removed his own robe to clothe a needy man and lived humbly in his home. Pilgrimage (Hajj) brings one to a state beyond self and possessions, merging wholly into the oneness of the Divine. When a man arrived for pilgrimage, the wise Rabia Adawiyya advised, "Scripture is like a physician's prescription, and practicing the Pillars is akin to taking the medicine. When it works, the illness heals, and once healed, one grows stronger." With health restored, one's strength endures.

The Prophet Muhammad once exerted himself so deeply in prayer that his feet became wounded. Wisdom and folly, in both saints and commoners, can be discerned in the practice of the Five Pillars.

End of "The Exposition on the Five Pillars of Rites."

The Exposition of the Five Pillars of Islam

by

Liu Zhi

Chinese Text

一性　第六十三章

小人、大人、同其理。

聖人、凡人、一其性。

唯欲窒而理蔽、習異而性分、則人品之相去遠矣。

五功者、所以合其理、而一其性也。

其殆天之機會、聖凡之市肆乎？

念之效、不起二念。

巴也贍德大賢、不計弟子名。

禮之效、受誇而無貶。

逆者、傷穆罕默德聖齒、反與之祝美。

齋之效、棄所欲、無往而不順。

賊害一補你爾秃花先賢九子、絶無一語。

課之效、一私不存。

穆罕默德至聖、脱袍濟貧、而坐守家庭。

朝之效、無己無物、而渾化於真一。

朝房來謁、勒畢爾賢者曰：經典如藥方、辦功如服藥、效即愈矣、愈而能服、保其強壯耳。

吾聖因副功拜而腿裂、聖凡知愚於五功中見之矣。

忠孝　第六十二章

五功、所以觀人於日用之間也。
事親而不勤五功、弗孝矣。
事君而不敬五功、弗忠矣。

處夫婦昆弟、而不修五功、弗義矣。
交朋友、接鄰里、而不以五功為觀法焉、不道矣。

耳聞、目睹、口言、鼻臭、手握、足行、念慮、思維、而不以五功為用焉、非禮矣。

是以至人之於五功也、曰日不間時、時不間息。

聖凡　第六十一章

五功、所以觀人者也。

若聖、若賢、若智、若愚、皆能不外五功、而自能成其為人。

聖之所以為聖者、全此五功也。

賢之所以為賢者、效此五功也。

智之所以為智者、知此五功也。

凡愚之所以為凡愚者、不知此五功也。

不知也者、不知其理也、不達其義也。

如飲食然、聖人治其味、而教人食者也。

賢人知其味、而食者也。

智者食之、而知其味者也。

凡愚不知其味、而不食者也。

即勉食之、而終不得其味也矣。

位育　第六十章

天之所以覆、地之所以載、日月之所以照臨、四時之所以運行、雨露時降、草木時生、鳥獸時育、萬物時成、皆所以培道之具也。人日享於其間、而不以修道為務者、亦有負造物之意矣。勤於天道、盡乎人倫、而位育之功成焉。

簡易　第五十九章

聖人之道、淺而深、近而遠。
其示人也簡易、其告人也諄切。
然而人不能盡其事、何也。
聖人示之簡、而人以為繁。
聖人示之易、而人以為難。
繁則病、難則勞。既病且勞、其何以行之哉。
是以行道之人、中途而廢者有之矣。
服教之人、沒身而失之者有之矣。

法程　第五十八章

聖人設教、將以為人陟天之階也。天位高遠、故其階次層疊、非一蹴而可盡也。

念、則欲登之意也。拜、則登之之法也。課、則絕物之牽也。齋、則忘己之有也。

絕物而忘己、斯至乎其天者矣。至乎其天、斯得朝覲之實者矣。

法聖　第五十七章

五功者、古今之定理也。
前聖之遺範、後聖之軌則、命於主、傳於聖、教於人、而人遵之。
是體主而法聖也。
祝乃德曰：聖人五功之全體、故為萬世觀法焉。

普概　第五十六章

五功、所以修身之道也。
其為理也、包乾括坤、無所遺。
其為教也、概聖越凡、無可免。
自少及老、統男與婦、而不容姑息。
其為禮制儀節也、體天地、象萬物、冒神祇、而力省乎於穆。

功用　第五十五章

五功之為用大也、通天人之幾、悉幽明之故、達性分之微、了生死之義。遠與於穆流行、而不蕩於虛淺。近於日用尋常、而益見其實際。顧其大而無外、細而無間、與時周旋、亙古今而不亂。

常德　第五十四章

五功者、成乎性命之德也、

全乎天人之義也、盡乎人事之常也。

其意大、其味良、民日用于其間、而莫之知也。

法象　第五十三章

五功之理、見於陰陽。
五功之道、充於天地。
五功之事、見於人身。
夫人身者、陰陽天地之大會也。
舍人身而別求陰陽天地者、未也。
是故人者、體乎天地之象者也、全乎陰陽之功者也、見諸陰陽天地之事者也。
欲言乎草木之生長、則人之生立肢體是。
欲言乎鳥獸之運動、則人之行止知覺是。
欲言乎神祇之靈明、則人之慧悟智解是。
欲言乎天之覆、地之載、則人之身心是。
欲言乎陰陽之消息、四時之變遷、則人之呼吸、盈虛、幼少、壯老是。
氣息如風雲、溫熱如炎火、鼻隆口凹如山谷、經分絡衍如河瀆、肉似土柔、骨如石堅。

天地之理、無不備於人。
天地之象、亦無不見於人。
此人之所以為天地之會、陰陽之本也。
故五功之效、特責在人、而不計他。

三極　第五十二章

天有五星、地有五行、人有五官、性有五德。
盡人之道、有五典。盡天之道、有五功。
夫五功包天地與人之事者也。
凡欲盡夫三極之道、而五功之禮、以一貫之矣。

功效　第五十一章

念主靜、以待天下之動、則無動而不收納於中矣。

禮主動、以歷天下之靜、則無靜而不遍閱於中矣。

齋無欲、則凡可欲不能亂吾衷、而愛惡公焉。

課無私、則凡所私不能為吾累、而得失等焉。

朝復本然、則理窮性盡、至於命矣。

天人脗合、而塞者通矣。

夫而後、聽非以耳、無所弗聽矣。

視非以目、無所弗視矣。

言不以口、動不以身、無思弗順、無感弗通。

夫而後、不思而得、無為而成。

知周有物、神應無方、大地之幾在我矣。

夫而後、以天用人、以人用天、天人盡妙、體用渾全、天道之本然、於茲可見矣。

若而人也天地莫能屆其量、日月莫能擬其明、鬼神莫能窺其事、算數不能紀其功。

（謂天地隱顯、形器不能為礙也。）

是五功之效也。聖人曰窮盡則主矣。

先賢曰功修既至、天地歸之、斯之謂也。

開官　第五十章

念、開口。
禮、潔身。
齋、開目。
課、開耳。
朝、開鼻。
是故阿丹一念而天地闢。
魯格茫恆念而微言通。
毋撒念四十日而對主言。吾聖一呻吟而天下奇才服。
是故阿丹再拜釋厄。
核子爾勤拜獲長生。爾撒日事禮拜、而肉身升天。
吾聖不因公誤拜、而全體成光、日下無影、蠅不沾衣、步履九霄之上。
是故易卜喇欣持齋、自見理世之幾微。
毋撒饑則見主。
吾聖得視墳形、見萬物性、玩天地始終如示掌、直見無何有之主。
是故哈灘善舍、聞百里之饑啼。
速來芒博施、解各類之蟲語。
吾聖九霄聞屐聲、熟羊告毒、婦啼而識其冤、日聆真主上諭。
是故葉爾孤白數千里聞衣香、以其心向之專也。
吾聖時聞妙世之香、得無臭之臭。蓋鼻乃天門、口為地闕也。
故氣運流行鼻之功。時新吐納口之事。五功盡妙、理象無遮。

忘想　第四十九章

念至無心、善念者也。
禮至無身、善禮者也。
齋至食色非欲、善齋者也。
課至聚斂非私、善課者也。
朝至無所趨蹌向背、善朝者也。
是故念不以心者、通身皆念之矣。
禮不以身者、動定皆禮之矣。
齋不以食色者、無欲非齋矣。
課不以財貨者、無私非課矣。
朝不以趨蹌向背者、無往非朝矣。
果能如是也、五官開焉、五德昭焉、五氣率從、而五事成焉。

屬意　第四十八章

念屬心、心屬微、其發脈在於口言、其於性分為仁、其於人道為孝、其於五行也、屬火。

禮屬身、身屬幾、其著事在於身行、其於性分為禮、於人道為弟、其於五行也、屬土。

齋屬意、意屬氣、戒於目見、謹於心思、其於性分為智、於人道為節、其於五行也、屬木。

課屬知、知屬血、施用得當、在於耳聽、其於性分為義、於人道為友誼、其於五行也、屬水。

朝屬性、性屬命、其為功也、具足一切功、施諸所有、

而至於鼻亦不臭香、其於性分為信、於人道為忠、其於五行也、屬金。

全體　第四十七章

五功、遍乎全體而無缺也。

有行於心者、有行於身者、有行於手足者、有行於首者、有行於耳目口鼻者。

蓋凡有一體、即有一體之過功、以滌其過也。云五功、約其總也。

無間　第四十六章

至人之於五功無間也。

有無心之念、不躬不叩之拜、不止食色之齋、不捐錢穀之課、不趨起蹌拱向之朝。

夫是者、五功之大者也。

民其能服事哉。細按此章、蓋言至人於未齋未拜之先、亦如齋拜之誠敬、此所以為無間也。

非謂不行五功、讀者審之。

必須細參徹悟、否則即誤非輕。

因斜者、杜撰者、依此據強辯、吾恐其傷己害衆也、哀哉哀哉。

然到此內功高品者、係刻到渾化於五功之裡者也、亦未廢其標表。

是以未聞古聖先賢、廢五功之標表也。視者慎之。慎之。

參化　第四十五章

五功治五官、五功發五德、五功盡五常、
五功讚五行、五功全五典。
五功參天地之化育、與陰陽同倫。

五息　第四十四章

五功有周旋不息之道焉、互相為始、互相為終、互相為體、互相為用、互相表裡、互相輔成、其由循還、莫可端窮。

五益　第四十三章

念格神、拜殺魔、齋息火、課息厄、朝絕牽繫。

旱雨　第四十二章

五功者、旱時雨、渴時泉、暗夜燈、茫津渡、炎午雲、療疾丹。古人遇艱難、未有不於此而得安者。

德門　第四十一章

五功者、入德之門、陟天之階、通微之徑、萬物之精、私欲之濾、氣質之礪、滌過之泉、濟海之航。修身養性、未有不由此而成功者。

五象　第四十章

拜、總萬物之象也。
齋、肖神祇察而不納。
課、肖天地施而不返。
朝、肖江河百匯歸宗。
念無肖、所以達乎於穆之精也。

故五功之中、惟念居首、惟念為大、惟念樞軸一切功。

誠意　第三十九章

念而不誠、臨拜而不恭、捐課而不樂、齋而不自省於時、朝而不精恪於其事。如之何。

念而不誠、猶未念也。
臨拜而不恭、猶未拜也。
捐課而不樂、猶未捐也。
齋而不自省於時、猶未齋也。
朝而不精恪於其事、猶未朝也。

聖人曰：萬務本乎心、成乎意。
是故鄉人砂成穀而錄功、篩核精修百年、一疑而失道。
修道者、可不謹其心意哉。

拜原　第三十八章

始晨拜者、阿丹也。
始晌拜者、易卜喇欣也。
始晡拜者、鬱訥思也。始昏拜者、爾撒也。
始夜拜者、母撒也。始衛特爾拜者、至聖穆罕默德也。
衆聖散見於前、吾聖集成於後、所謂道全德備、卓越於千古者也。

儀象　第三十七章

叩首、草木根地之象也。

鞠躬、鳥獸負天之象也。

跪坐、山陵盤踞之象也。

站立、頂天立地之象也。

周旋升降、陰陽消息、日月運行之象也。

是故拜也者、冒天地之全分者也。

禮數　第三十六章

夫拜有儀也、有義也。
以七天之理、合而為一拜之儀。
主制十二、典禮十二、聖則二十有八、體天輪之常轉、包日月之運行。
括五行之深義、總萬類之全功、此拜之儀也。

求滌己身之罪業、默祝國家之太平、思親恩而感師訓。
念友誼以及群生、此拜之義也。

夫拜有數也。一日之中、三十二鞠躬、六十四叩頭、一百七十八讚、
十二抬手、十七跪、三十二起、二十七獻、左右顧者十一、宣諭五、
讚禮五、合一日而為數、三百八十有四。
此合天地初開、日分之理數也。

衆義　第三十五章

拜必俱衆、何。

民務紛紜、心意叢雜、雖臨拜、其衷不能無擾也。惟入寺俱衆而禮之、進趨謹畏、瞻闞凜然、威儀濟濟、班次嚴肅、怠慢之容自怯、誠敬之心油然。如此乃得拜功之福。

聖人曰：俱衆禮一拜、七十倍獨禮之功。故曰：鄰寺者無拜、惟於寺。

七日一聚、何。

天地之數七也。以七天之禮、合而為一拜之儀、此紀天地之數也。

一年二會、何。

會也者、自萬歸一之義也。於一年而重之、一為開會、畢天道之會也。一為祀會、畢人道之會也。

聚會　第三十四章

俱人而拜之謂衆、七日一禮之謂聚、二節之禮之謂會。一日五衆、七日一聚、一年二會。

會者、會一切聚也。聚者、聚一切衆也。衆者、俱一切人也。會之為言會也、會其繁而統於一也。會統聚、聚統衆、衆統人、人統身、身統性、性統心、是為理會、大於象會。象會以時、理會無時、是以至人一息二會。

五限　第三十三章

時念、何也。心之功也。

心無止息、念亦無止息也。

隱動幾微之際、理欲善惡之根、頃有忽焉、終身之禍。

惟以時念防之、則心有操存而不放矣。

日禮五時、何也。禮、身之功也。

身多營為、當暇時而拜也。曉發、政未起、暇矣、當拜。

日仄政歇、身暇矣、當拜。方晡、百務咸畢、暇矣、當拜。

昏夕、百務咸皆歸藏、暇矣、當拜。

及夜、萬彙寢寐、身心俱暇矣、當拜。

若當暇時而不暇、惟身心是務者、是逆命而願已也。

一日五時、取五中之義也。晨、是夜交晝之中。昏、是晝交夜之中。

晌、是晝之中。宵、是夜之中。晡、居四時之中。

經曰：爾民禮拜、務守其中。此中謂歟。一曰、古之聖人始禮之拜、即當此五時也。

至今守之無改、以追法往聖也。歲齋一月、何。齋、性之功。

性無為、而人之生也、罔不有為。家國之役、農賈之勞、所不免焉。

惟於一年之中、齋一月。罷工停政、斯於民無難矣。逾歲一課、何。本、財貨之功也。

一年四時、生植營藝、出入籌計、而財貨之盈縮定矣。

然後計其定數而捐之、斯不損其本也。

於四十取一、何也。萬物之數、至四十而盈也。衰多益寡之義也。

一生一朝、何。朝總身心財貨、且去家國之功也。是功於民為難、故惟一生一朝而可矣。

苟無能焉、朝於其國可也。期年一大朝、七日一小朝、聖人之教、切而不迫也。

朝證　第三十二章

理境之於人、若朝堂之於天下也。
無處不通、無人不可至、而惟人背之、則日趨於遠。
或向之而功程未盡、終不能到。是朝堂無阻於人、而人自阻也。
朝堂無隔於人、而人自隔也。

理境於人亦然、無人不可至此理、無處不可見此理。
而惟人之向背不同、功夫各別、故有聖凡賢愚之差異也。
理本通而人自塞、理本明而人自晦。
苟能一日返身而向之、而歸於一原焉、則何聖凡賢愚之別乎。

朝堂有遠近、理無遠近。朝堂有方位、理無方位。
期月而朝、形跡之朝也。返身而誠、則時時朝、處處朝。

時時朝、則無念而不以主為思維。
處處朝、則無動而不以主所命我者為遵守。
念拜、齋課、皆以一朝而包完。身心、性命、皆以一朝而修盡。
忠孝、節義、皆以一朝而周全。天道、人道、皆盡於一朝之功。

故曰：朝者百功之總會也。
苟於身心之間、有一念一動之違於理、即為背真、即為朝之義無有矣。
是故觀人之朝者、觀於其日用工夫而已矣。觀於其舉止動定而已矣。

朝理　第三十一章

朝曰歸、義旨盡矣。歸者、人所公欲、而萬物自然之情也。

旅人之還家曰歸、使臣之復命曰歸、鳥之返林、魚之下淵、百川之匯海也、皆回歸。

歸、蓋出於人物之自然、而無強勉之情也。

欲歸而遏之不使歸、何不自然之甚。

歸焉而未止於其境、何不自安之甚。

雖然人之處於外也、必有所為而來、底事未盡、則亦難言乎歸。

人之處世、旅之寓也、將必歸、必有所為而來也。

盡其事、而後乃可歸。聖人盡其事歸矣、而憫人之弗歸、復作法以導之歸。

賢者效之、而率人歸。智者從之歸。

愚人不欲歸。惟嗜欲是戀、漸至流蕩忘返、而終於不知歸。

朝覲一功、乃指其歸境、而勉之歸也。夫歸、自然之事、何須勉。

上人不勉而歸。中人勉之而歸。下愚勉之而亦不歸。

此下愚終成其為下愚也、其不若物類也甚矣。

朝義　第三十章

人惟懷土之念深、則契道之念淺。

朝覲者、絕域登途、去所貪戀、以近其本原也。

夫朝覲之人、割愛離家、崎嶇跋涉、而後乃詣其境。

則凡修道之人、亦必熔克己私、勤修苦行、而後乃還其真。

此借有形之朝、以起無形之朝也。

善朝者、身向而心亦向之矣。

遠其私欲之鄉、逾一切好惡之界、至禮義之闕、新歸潔之沐浴、脫人欲衣、服天理戒、登明識山、會常安郊。宰氣欲性、然後入親主之禁、所撫機微之懸石、拜伏於契合之聖位、即接渾化之天房矣。

外之所朝者、似乎趨蹌之跡猶存。

而內之所朝者、渾乎真宰之體為一矣。修道之功、豈復有過於此者哉。

經曰：棄爾來。謂棄爾己私、來於天理、此朝覲之實義也。

朝法　第二十九章

夫朝者、五功之總歸、而天人之大會也。

念不輟於心、詞不輟於口。拜焉、謹趨蹌、而昭對越。

齋焉、謹外制內、而制身心於無為之境。

財不用、私不減、稱其所有而力行之。

自居而途、自近而遠、割愛離鄉、崎嶇跋涉、功行之中、莫勤於此、莫勞於此。

愛焉而不自愛也。

毋謂觀瞻、毋謂遠離、毋謂身至而即為功。

嚴防乎戒、縝密乎事、內外精嚴、極盡乎誠敬而已。

朝儀　第二十八章

朝覲者、身心財貨、均至乎主、而以返其初也。

天方其生人之始地也。

期月而朝、至關受戒、沐浴易服、不飾裝、不宰牲、先朝謁。

飲曰飲性、厥明大會彌拿（墨克南郊）。

王帥群寮士庶。晨駐而里付堤（山名）、夕駐母子德里付（山名）、味爽歸彌拿。

大射、開戒、宰牲、沐浴、盛服、佩香、乃入覲撫石、遊庭七匝（天房）、

臨位禮拜、致祈祝、出登索法（山名）仰天朝厥（即天房）。

而讚、而頌、而告、下徑白土泥川、趨於兩墊之間、

登墨而禨（山名）、事如索法（山名）、復入拜闕、如前儀、歸彌拿、

厥明復射、翌日終射、謁陵、探泉、歸復辭朝。

課證 第二十七章

捐課、將以去其私執之心也。

私物之心尚存、執己之心未化、何有於課哉。

然非欲盡舍其有也。

厭求而不慍、多索而益歡、財則財之、力則力之、若一身之恤苦、不立彼我之見、斯可矣。

抑得之若寄、失之若返、餘則以為禍累、不足以為福美。

若負擔涉險、然惟輕減而願、斯可矣。抑衆人之私在財貨、大人之私在有己。

存一物於心、留一見於己、猶未課也。身世全舍、福報無取、則善課者焉。

課理　第二十六章

人之所本有者、德性耳。

一切外物、培德之具也。

即身形亦具也。培以生之、而反害之、則非具矣、累矣。

不惟外物為累、即身形亦累矣。

上人不為所累、故雖身命亦其非有。

中人知其累而能舍之。

下此者則執之而不舍、終被其累而弗覺也。

捐課一法、其示人去外有之私、而用其本有之德性耳。

課義 第二十五章

課者、體主、愛人而忘己、忘物之大法也。

真主至仁、施而不斷。吾能施之、是體主之仁也。

民吾一身、理宜同愛、而分甘普利、是愛民如身也。

舍其己有、猶忘己有也。不私其物、猶忘物也。

人惟私己之心太甚、故仁愛公義之心不起。

一舉課、而四義全焉。

課法　第二十四章

衷多益寡、克己分甘、仁者之為也。

匿於毫未、則毀於全功。

必也為道而捐、樂而出之、不懷恩心、不眩善名。

挾私而與、其猶挾私而匿。

勞來賜贈、不作課功、義俠修建、不入課例。謹之謹之、得其人而後與。

慎之慎之、度其可而後受。不稽而與、與之過也。朦溷而受、受之過也。

課儀 第二十三章

課者、以其財貨用于主也。

財貨主無所用、而以與貧、由之乎用于主也。

滿貫者、捐其四十之一。

金、銀、錢、貨、牛、羊、駝、馬、果穀、生産、各有定例、依律清算無隱、一年一課。

受給者：貧乏、良人。先親後疏、先近後遠、餘課納官入庫、賑饑養學。

非其人不給、非其人不受、給受之間、有大謹焉。

聖人曰：凡物有課、有所能而施之、以濟不能也。

財富者利濟貧乏、學優者導化愚頑、言美者釋訟解爭、力強者扶危助弱、廣修屋廈、以延賓客、多備器用、以應借貸。皆課之義也。

齋證 第二十二章

僅能止食色、而不能忘食色、非齋也。

僅能戒非為、而不能絕非念、非齋也。

僅能守齋、而不見其為齋之效、亦非齋也。

願無食色、幾忘食色者矣。

畏有非念、幾忘非念者矣。

厭離情欲、樂乎天命、幾見其為齋之效者矣。

聖人曰：齋以鎔氣質也。

即如鎔金、去其雜而聚其散。齋矣、氣質未絕、紛散未聚、猶未齋也。

遠離食色、齋之次也。制欲檢行、齋之上也。

已私克盡、物我全忘、齋之制也。

故曰：齋以絕物也、絕其外物、化其己私。而不納一物於心焉、斯可謂之齋矣。

齋理 第二十一章

食色以生、生以為道也、不得已也。

求道者減食色、至於棄食色、皆視食色為累者也、皆以不食不色為樂者也。

且食色後天之需、日逐於食色、則日沉淪於後天、而於先天日漸蔽塞而不通矣。

抑其後天之情、示以先天之性、而後憶乎先天之景況、則幾復乎先天矣。

先天復而於真主本然何間焉。

故曰：齋屬予、予報之。親切至矣。

齋義 第二十章

一切不善、嗜欲為之先、氣血為之乘。

守齋則嗜欲遏、氣血羸、而非為妄作、無所從起矣。

德性所以養心、而能潤及其身。飲食所以養身、而能累及其心。

齋止食飲、以抑氣質、以強其心也。

心強則明、明則私欲化、而真性見矣。

聖人曰：萬物有課、夫齋、氣血之課也。

經曰：主謂爾撤、饑則見、孤則合。謂饑於食而飽於德、則性見。

孤於己而復於禮、則真合也。一塵不染、一私不立、謂之孤。

齋法 第十九章

夫齋者、制欲檢行、以謹身心、於無妄之法也。

目不妄視、耳不妄聽、口不妄言、心不妄思、手不妄取與、足不妄步趨。

塵欲之事遠絕、道義之事精虔。

徒謹嗜欲而不去邪妄、非齋也。

知謹邪妄而不輟食色、非法也。

蓋食色者、嗜欲之母也。不輟食色、是不能制嗜欲者也。

不能制嗜欲、其與齋乎何有。

聖人曰：齋、非僅止食色也、務齋諸耳目身心。

又曰：嗜欲之情、人禽共之。人之所以異於禽獸者、能制其情耳。

齋儀　第十八章

齋者、性乎主也。

歲齋一月、曉初而食、日沒而開。

一日之中、不茹水穀、不近女色、百務皆息。

諸念不生、民不列市、官不聽訟、君不設朝、不行野。

或處於家、或守於寺、惟省躬滌過、獨契真宰無已。

聖人曰：齋無為之功也。罷工停政、以重其事焉。

拜證 第十七章

拜、言乎順也。無乎不順、則無乎不拜。順乎主、即拜乎主也。

夫順主有二：順其命令之當然、順之表也。順其本然之德性、順之裡也。

表裡當順、則表裡皆拜者也。無時不順、則時時皆拜者也。

主命吾念、則念之。命吾拜、則拜之。非以念拜為功也、以順為功也。

非以不念、不拜為過也、以不順為過也。蓋主命如是、即當如是、是為順也。

主無方位、吾亦不以方位拘。主無形體、吾亦不以形體礙。

主無聲色嗅味、吾亦不以聲色嗅味而迷障。

一念本然、安於其境、聽其自然而已矣。

順焉而不拜、則順無效。拜焉而不順、則拜無功。

拜於其時、順於無間、斯之為真拜者也。

拜理 第十六章

凡屬有物、不出二端、通也、礙也。

通也理也、礙也象也。滯於象者、礙於理。復於理者、通於象。

然非去象以求理也。能通於理、礙即為通。不通於理、通亦成礙。

人也者、理與象、全體聚合之名也。

日羈於象、則無由復於通。不特身形不能復於通、即性靈亦不能復於通。何也。

靈為形役矣。日求於理、而象不能為其礙。

不特靈性不能為所礙、即身形亦不能為所礙。何也。形為靈超矣。

靈為形役、即通而成礙。

形為靈超、即礙而成通。拜也者、形為靈超之妙用也、即礙還通之佳境也。

果能至於此境矣、則生死不以為生死、而知有不生不死者在。

嗜欲不以為嗜欲、而明有無嗜無欲者在。

夫是以不免於生死、亦為超脫生死者。夫是以不離於嗜欲、而為棄絕嗜欲者。

象者化矣、礙者通焉。經喻諄諄、教人禮拜、欲其即礙返通而已矣。

流通則漫越寓、顯著則生滅明晦寓、運化則動靜往復寓。

凡此諸情、皆非本有、情為性障、性為情掩、違理畔道、日逐於遠。

拜也者、超乎情障、而復乎原有也。

原有復則新有無存、其本然之謂也。

故站、頂天立地、人之象也。

躬、負天向地、鳥獸之象也。

叩、身首代地、草木之象也。

跪、端坐靜居、山礦與地之象也。

升上降下、水與火之象也。

運行往來、氣之象也。

由動而止於靜、復初之象也。

舉諸象而意示之、依層次而度越之、斯歸原近主之實義也。

拜義 第十五章

禮拜、近主之階也、歸原之徑也。

人之生也、自理世而之象世、歷多境界。

每歷一境、即染一象、而與其初位、即遠一層。

層隔萬疊、大端在七:氣、水、火、土、金、木、活也。

由理之氣、有運化象。

由氣之火、有顯著象。

由火之水、有流通象。

由水之土、有凝聚象。

由土之金、有固結象。

由金之木、有長發象。

由木之活、有運行象。

象象相資、諸情遂寓。

運行則嗜欲寓、長發則生死寓、固結則離合寓、凝聚則渙散寓、

拜法　第十四章

拜必恭、心必虔。不恭不虔、與不拜等。時必殷、日無間。殷而無間、乃作成功。

夫拜、主命也。時至身必至、時至而身不至、是私身而慢主也。

身至心必至、身至而心不至、是虛文而無實也。慢主者逆、無實者謬、逆則禍、謬則不登。

是故禮拜必神存心臨、內慄外莊、毋外慮、毋旁顧、毋搔首、毋舉足、毋作聲。故犯者復禮。

聖人曰：拜主如見主、雖爾不見、主實見之。

拜儀 第十三章

拜者、身乎主也。

一日五時、參禮以衆。時：晨、晌、晡、昏、夜是也。

時各有數：晨禮四拜、晌禮十拜、晡禮四拜、昏禮五拜、夜禮九拜。

拜有四儀：立、躬、叩、跪。立則端身正面、拊手齊足、目矚叩所。

躬則曲身懸首、平脊捉膝、目矚足。叩則身首匍匐、鼻額著地、懸肘懸腹、目矚鼻端。

跪則端坐、沉沉、默首撫膝、目矚懷。合數儀而成一拜、全數拜而成一禮。

禮有條例：沐浴、盛服、潔處、正時、正向、立意。

一日五禮、七日一聚、一年二會。惟大人有明禮、有夜功。明禮兩拜、夜功無數。

經曰：爾民禮拜、務守其中。中者、時中之謂也。

聖人曰：順與逆、無以分也、惟以拜。時至而不拜、逆矣夫。

念證 第十二章

有心之念、以人念主也。

無心之念、以主念主也。

念主以人、有工夫、有時際。念主以主、則無時無地、而非念主矣。則無動無思、而非念主矣。

苟有一念一動之不合於道、則是為有時際。

而以主念主者、動止非我、渾乎無間、憶慮消忘、肆應周徧、斯為以主念主者也。

故曰：維念無方、居不昧念也。起不忘念也。接物以正、待人以忠、念也。

經云：經營政治、農圃術數而以道、皆念也。

聖人曰：不念而事事必逆、念而不肖於行、念乎哉。

念理 第十一章

人與主無間也、而必屬念於主者、正以示其無間耳。

人以人為物、而不知無物之非主。人以物為幻、而不知無幻之非真。

念人、念物、則只見人、物、而不見主。惟一念專屬於主、則物我無存、本然獨湛矣。

經曰：真主臨人、切於心命。

又曰：念毋二、敬毋二、奉事毋二。二之云者、將以他物二於主也、二甚於逆。

念義 第十章

念、示不忘也。不忘吾之本原也。

身之所生、性之所自、造物之本然也。

本然至善、念之則無惡。本然至清、念之則無染。本然至真、念之則無妄。

夫念至於無惡、無染、無妄、即還本原之境矣。

聖人曰：念則超焉。

超乎物我、還乎本然、是為原始返終之義。

念法　第九章

心猶鑑也。面於此、必背於彼。

天理也、人欲也、心之面背不常。

面於天理、則人欲不入。面於人欲、則天理不存。

是非之判、善惡之端、皆造化於此。危哉、微哉、敬哉、慎哉。

一念正、終身之福。一念不正、終身之禍。

敬肆關頭、如防激湍、如羈劣馬。念茲在茲、時加省察。

聖人曰心昏如鑑垢、念以磨之。

念儀　第八章

念者、心乎主也。時省於懷、常注於口、永佩乎身、存誠執敬、歌功頌德。

凡屬言行、標理中節、惟恐一動離乎道。心念不忘、口念不輟。

經曰：興居寢食、惟念念哉。

又曰念主者、主念之。

念主則無過、主念則無虞。自我勤慎、自主祐之。

正變 第七章

人稟四行而生、五行而成。賦質之初、精為水、血為土、溫暖為火、運化者為氣。

成形以後、氣與火合而生木、土與水合而生金。

木性以滋長養、金性以滋堅明、並精液之水、溫暖之火、骨肉之土、此之為五行、而氣則主乎其中、即靈覺之謂也。

夫五者、各一其性、各一其德。

火性向上、其德高明、水性向下、其德謙遜。木性條暢、其德直樸。

金性堅定、其德穩重、土性藏育、其德靜順。夫德者、必惟氣之得養、乃各用乎其中正也。

苟失其養、則中者反而為倚、正者變而為偏矣。

是故高明、則變而為強暴、而好欲滋焉。

謙遜、則變而為阿從、而淫蕩滋焉。穩重、則變而為固執、而膠泥滋焉。

直樸、則變而為頑冥、而愚魯滋焉。

靜順、則變而為遲鈍、而怠惰滋焉。五性一變、私欲之所從生也、萬惡之所從出也。

是皆由於氣之失養、而各反乎其中也。五功者、所以養氣之法、而致五性於至中者也。

以上七章、總述五功之由。其下二十五章、分述五功之理、末後三十一章、發明五功之義。通記六十三章、以取聖壽之紀云。

心性 第六章

性分之內、復有五德焉、仁也、義也、禮也、智也、信也。五者所以公乎世者也。

心分之內、有五德焉、喜也、怒也、愛也、惡也、欲也。五者所以存乎己者也。

知分之內、有五德焉、憶也、記也、悟也、籌也、運也。五者所以用乎世者也。

三分之德、務適於中、有一偏焉、其道反失。五功者、所以救其偏而歸於中也。

內德　第五章

人有內德五焉、　心也、性也、知也、幾也、微也。

性所以生、心所以覺、知所以用、幾則心之動、微則心之隱。（已發為之機、未發為之微。）

五者本至善、而受於造物者也。

第私欲漓乎性、是非撓乎心、氣質蔽乎知、

謀慮亂乎幾、喜怒得喪動乎微、本善者遂流於不善矣。

五功之理、所以湔其私、正其氣、平其是非、

定其謀慮、而約束於喜怒得喪之際者也。

外官　第四章

五官為用、各有德性具焉。

而人未能盡其善也。

口具能言之德、

耳具能聽之德、

目具能視之德、

鼻具能嗅之德、

身具能取與動止之德。

德無不善、而或用之不善、則德性喪矣。

五功者、拯其既喪之德、而亦保其德不至喪也。

愛惡　第三章

耳之於聲也、

目之於色也、

鼻之於嗅也、

口之於味也、

身之於觸也、

雖各異其官、而愛美惡惡、則無不同。

夫無愛無惡、無美無惡、渾然天理者、公德也。

受其所愛、而弗審所當愛、惡其所惡、而弗審所當惡、私德也。

愛而知其惡、惡而知其美者、明德也。

五功之為治於人也者、克去己私、復還明德、以歸於大公而已。

本義 第二章

天道人心、妙而通也。

真主以一理賦物、而人之稟受不同、故有聖凡之別。

聖人以道道物、故道無不明。

凡人以物物道、則道有所蔽、故不能復其理、而復還其本初也。

因是主命五功、示人修道之方、將以開蔽通塞、指其來路、而導之歸焉。

功以五者何。人之心性相偕、如鎖鑰然。

其耳目口鼻身、既有聲色臭味觸五者之染、即生愛惡五者私欲之簧。

簧鑰交締、牢莫可解、必須按鑰製匙、絲杪恰合、以為啟折之備、則簧與鑰、脫然解矣。

一身有五者之累、亦必以五法對治之、累可漸釋、則心明性見、而道明矣。

此五法之所以為修道之切要也。

原始 第一章

形氣章矣、天道隱矣。

氣稟日生、真理晦矣。

明者蔽、純者雜、而通者塞矣。

人於天命根源、罔知所自而返焉。

聖教五功、念禮齋課朝、示人修道、而返乎其本初也。

念在知所歸、禮在踐所歸之路、齋以絕物、課以忘己、朝以復命而歸真。

修此、而天道盡矣。

明教之禮

流教分途久、清真理獨深。
三才憑造化、五府任陶鈞。
無極緣何極。有神匪白神。
靜參玄奥旨、誠奉厥維寅。

明教之用

不染維清潔、有源理白真。
誠心純終始、一篤顯微伸。
忠孝無他計、解推不厭頻。
服膺匪有得、願共寶奇珍。

序

自有太極、而兩儀生焉。
自有兩儀、而四象立焉。
有四象、即有五行。
五行者、相生相剋者也、而清真教規、亦有五焉、　念也、禮也、齋也、課也、朝也。
此亦猶五行之不可減者也、而生剋之義亦寓焉。

生者、本然之性、由此而生也。
剋者、繼起之私、因此而去也。
總存乎人之用意何如耳。
意存乎真、則行此五者、自見其真、意存乎文、則行此五者、僅見其文。
所謂仁者見之謂之仁、智者見之謂之智、深者自深、淺者自淺、是也。

今劉一齋先生於五功之義、一一窮究其源、而又推類以及餘、
使後之學者反復尋求、身心一片、於其所已言者、固可了然於心、
而於其所未言者、亦未始不可觸類而旁通、則所謂五功者、功豈止於五哉。

天數五、地數五、五位相得而各有合、凡天地之數五十有五者、
莫不由五而推、則體此五者、精察而力行之、
而真積力久、自可下學而上達、而約之又約、以至相忘於無言、
此又先生之所厚望於天下、天下其無忘先生所用意也云。

時　康熙四十九年庚寅三月燈下識
眷教弟拜楷拜撰

五功釋義

劉智

The Exposition of the Five Pillars of Islam

by

Liu Zhi

Chinese Text